Thankful for
all you do!

Catie Hugh

MARRY ME FIRST

Who's waiting at the end of your aisle?

CATIE HUGHES

WESTBOW
PRESS®
A DIVISION OF THOMAS NELSON
& ZONDERVAN

WestBow Press books may be ordered through booksellers or by contacting:

WestBow Press
A Division of Thomas Nelson & Zondervan
1663 Liberty Drive
Bloomington, IN 47403
www.westbowpress.com
844-714-3454

ISBN: 978-1-6642-5565-4 (sc)
ISBN: 978-1-6642-5566-1 (hc)
ISBN: 978-1-6642-5564-7 (e)

Library of Congress Control Number: 2022900944

Print information available on the last page.

WestBow Press rev. date: 02/14/2022

Contents

Contents

Dedication

THIS BOOK IS DEDICATED TO MY PARENTS, MOM, YOU ARE MY BEST friend and mentor. Dad, you have shown me what it looks like for a godly man to genuinely love, value, and honor the women in his life. Mrs. Alicia and Scott, you both poured into my life in more ways than you could ever know. To my friends who encouraged me along the way, and finally, to my favorite person in the whole wide world; you know who you are.

About Me

I LOVE READING. I LOVE HOW I CAN ENCOUNTER SUCH THOUGHTS and opinions that can challenge me and change me in ways I never expected. There is so much beauty in wisdom and in the willingness to let the knowledge of others guide me. Throughout my literary journey, I have found many amazingly talented writers with so much wisdom to share with the world.

Multigenerational wisdom provides such beauty to our world. It opens us up to encounter and learn about experiences in life that we have yet to even begin to walk through. Words spoken by previous generations provide security, direction, and peace to some of the unknowns.

How older authors form their thoughts and opinions and make a more precise understanding for the generations to come is so needed and beautiful. I have found, however, one similarity throughout my journey in life. I have read many books by authors who refer to one specific time in their lives, but I have not read many books in which the author is currently walking through that time. Please do not misinterpret what I am saying. There is always more to learn and so much we can see when we walk away and look back at past moments in our lives from a distant perspective. But what can we learn from someone who shares their heart in that present moment? Such transparency and vulnerability are open to us when we can listen and see someone currently sharing what they are going through and how they are processing it.

Those who have already gone through this portion of their journey can encourage and stand as a reminder that others can and will make it during struggles. They stand as promises that the situations and hard times can and will end in beauty, if given the opportunity. But on the flip side, there is something powerful and timely behind the transparency in the present. There are times in this walk when it is hard to see beyond the current moment, and words and affirmations of those who have made it before us seem so distant. Even in good faith and efforts, other words of encouragement and hope can seem so far away from our present situations. There have been so many days when I feel like I am the only one feeling this way, which I know is not valid; however, many times, in the rough portions of our journeys, this feels like reality.

I wrote this book with one thing before me: transparency. I wrote with honesty that life is not rainbows and butterflies all the time, and I wrote with humility in acknowledging I have not always been in a close place with the Lord, and my journey has been continual ups and downs. Brokenness, heart ties, and discouragement have left me feeling hopeless at many points in my walk.

I do not know many, younger twenties authors writing about life and God, so I thought I might give this a go. I decided to let people into the mess of my life and to speak to how God has helped me sort it out along the way. I would have loved to have had a book that helped me to see I wasn't alone and that helped encourage me through some of the most challenging years of life, college, and adulthood.

So here it goes: a young college graduate, writing about life, love, and God and how those collided beautifully and messily to change my perspective and my walk along the way.

Logically, I feel that the best way to start a book is to give some context to the person who is sharing her opinions, experiences, and walk with you in the first place. I will fit my twenty-five years of life into the following paragraphs to help you understand more of who Catie Hughes is and the story of why her heart is so passionate for people who experience what she has and is participating in life.

I grew up in a small one-traffic-light town, as a privileged young girl who thrived in knowing everyone within her community. Small communities can play a significant part in molding you, if you let it. Such an environment can be good or bad; mine was good. I could tell you everything there is to know about that little town. I could show you the hidden hiking trails, beautiful mountain overlooks, the school with the cow pasture behind the football field, the only Sonic Drive-In in town, the pizza place with the best cheese sticks, and so much more. Within a small community, time allows you to discover the hidden gems that no one else knows about or cares to find. Isn't it funny how something seemingly insignificant and small to others can be considered beautiful and unique to you? Once you get to know a place, the good seems to outweigh the bad. It was a town that everyone dreamed of getting out of, but not me. I didn't mind small-town life. I liked knowing everyone's name and story. I loved being known and recognized by my kindergarten teacher or high school principal.

Surprisingly, my small town also included a small school. This school often was the brunt of surrounding schools' jokes, but I didn't mind. I loved my school. I knew everyone in my graduation class of 150. Most of us had grown up together, going to the same school with each other since kindergarten. I remember seeing the cows graze just past the football field through the school windows. They seemed so small in comparison to the beautiful mountains that stood behind. That may have been why I loved my school; it helped remind me of the beauty in life. Small-town life allowed me to hold close my best moments and some of my darkest, all the while pointing to a more remarkable story of beauty. I found myself surrounded by great friends, teachers, and family who came together so beautifully for me during those hard times, and I know that is part of why I ended up where I am now, writing this book.

It does not take long for anyone to realize how much I love my family. I am blessed with a fantastic family. They are not perfect by any means, but let's be honest: whose family is? I was raised by two amazing parents who created a household that served the Lord. They modeled the characteristics of godly people. They gave without expecting anything in return, tithed without anger or resentment, cared for people, listened to people, and, most important, *loved* people. They showed me, from an early age, how to love with a godly love, one that cannot be defiled and one that breaks through the enemy's darkness like cream pouring into black coffee. It's a love that gives, expecting nothing in return, no price tag, just unending.

I have two older siblings. My sister, Trina, is an incredible lawyer. My brother, Joshua, is a mechanical genius who could outshine almost any mechanic since he was a teenager. Both of my siblings are highly intelligent, and school was never too hard for them. They understood things without much effort; that, unfortunately, is not my story. God knew I needed an extra push to have the work-hard mentality instilled in me because, unfortunately, information did not remain in my head as easily. I had to work hard for every little piece of intelligence and wisdom that my brain retained. There were multiple days and nights of studying, studying, and more studying to do well in my academic career. I have never been the kid to look over notes ten minutes before the test and ace it. I am a student who does well, but only because I studied for five hours. I don't resent that aspect about myself. It helped to mold me into a determined worker who is willing to do whatever it takes to accomplish my heart goals. My best may not be what I hoped for, but I can always say that I did my best.

Along with a blessed home life, I also was raised in a church radical after God. My children's pastors, Mrs. Alicia and Scott, taught me about a relationship with the Lord from a young age—but not just a relationship. They taught us kids how to have an *intimate* relationship with the Lord. They taught us that we didn't have to wait until we were older to lay on our faces before the throne, lead dramas and worship, or pray for each other. They instilled in me godly confidence and hunger that remain today. Even when I was younger, I knew I did not want to be a mediocre Christian.

I wanted God to use me whenever God saw fit. I knew if I were willing and available, God would use me, just as He did the adults around me. That understanding never left me.

We overlook children in so many ways in our walks with God. We teach them the essential scriptures, but we often say it's too complicated for them to understand deep relationships. People poured into me the foundation of never being too young to have a deep connection with God, and that has only grown stronger over time. I knew that I didn't have to be this or that to be used; I just had to be available. I wanted to find God in a more profound way, and God always found me. It was like an addiction when I was little—enough was never enough. It's a good thing that I serve an eternal God because the wonders of His beautiful mysteries always leave me awestruck and wanting more.

As for my daily life, I am just an ordinary college student. I love any type of coffee made available to me. I am also a procrastinator, something that college has helped me to master. Book report due tomorrow night? Cool; I'll read the book tomorrow afternoon. Thirty-page paper due Monday? I'll get right on that Saturday night.

As of this writing, I am about to start my senior year as an intercultural studies major; I want to work in other places than just the States. I am finishing my bachelor's degree, but I still don't know what the future will look like—and I am slowly concluding that it is OK. It has taken a lot of time for me to get to the point of being OK with the unknown because I like having plans. And it has taken a lot of stretching and growing pains to get me to this point of embracing the beautiful, yet utterly terrifying unknown.

I dream about what I will do in life, but to say I have it planned out and know exactly what it will look like would be a lie. I pray that it will involve working with kids in orphanages, loving them, and telling them how loved and cherished they are. I hope that my arms will do more than just type theology papers. I want to embrace the world around me with a love that pours from the depths of my heart, just like Jesus. I want to speak words of life, love, and truth as

I live a life, fighting for those who are silenced today. I want to have eyes that see the brokenness, pain, and reality around me; I want to let that penetrate deep within my heart to move it to action. I don't want to be another Christian who just gets through life; I want to be active. I want to be involved in the world in which I live. I want to live into a bigger purpose than I could ever envision for myself. My dreams and hopes go in so many directions, and it is hard to see how they will connect at times, but it is OK. This life may be a weird road filled with twists and turns, and I may not know what the results of my walk will look like, but that is also OK. I am in great hands.

I felt the need to step out of my comfort zone and share what God has spoken to me, as well as some of my stories along the way. So here we go.

Introduction

I AM SO VERY IN LOVE WITH A MAN, AND NOTHING THAT ANYONE does or says will change that. My mind is made up. I have chosen to spend forever with Him, and this is just the beginning of our journey. I am beyond obsessed with Him, and, quite frankly, He is beyond obsessed with me. I can't get Him out of my mind. Every morning when I wake up, I'm constantly thinking about it. My mind acts like a hamster running on a wheel. My thoughts for Him are continual, quick, and persistent. I get excited to wake up in the morning because sleep no longer parts our conversations with one another. Best of all, not one single morning goes by that He doesn't tell me how much He loves me. He constantly tells me He loves me. He whispers it to me in the chaos, He sings it over me in the silence, and He continually declares it over me in my questions and disbelief. He reminds me repeatedly how much He loves me in such beautiful and intimate ways.

My family finds rest, knowing they never have to worry whether this man will honor me, cherish me, protect me, and provide for me. They know that not only does He love me passionately, but He honors me fiercely. He celebrates who I am as a woman and honors who I have been called to be within the church. There are so many unique qualities about Him that an entire book could not begin to give Him justice. He is an incredible planner; He has our entire future planned out. I don't have to worry about whether I will have what I need to make it through life because He is such a great provider to everyone He loves. Even if I cannot plan for everything, I know He does. Life throws me curveballs, and sometimes I really mess up, yet it doesn't surprise Him. He sees me, He hears me in the mess I am in, and He still has a plan amid it all. He sits with me in my mess, and when the time comes, He is there with arms open to my pain and brokenness and offers a hand, willing to help me get up to move forward. There is no doubt in my mind that He will always take care of me.

He knows me so well. Sometimes He even knows what I need, even when I cannot recognize it for myself. He can read me like a book. It is a vulnerable and intimidating place to be, but He quickly shows that I can trust Him with all of me. The beautiful thing is that there is no pretending when I am around Him. And in the days when I feel tempted to hide myself away, He provides the release to let it go and show him the real me. I am confident that there are even times when He knows what I think before I think it! I don't try to withhold my whole heart from Him anymore. I can't fool Him because He has always seen my heart; He saw it from the beginning.

There is such beauty in that place of raw intimacy and transparency, as scary as that feels at times. It is so comforting to know that someone can understand me to the very depths of myself and still love me with such a passion. He loves the places within me that I am scared to face. How does He do it? He loves me despite it all. Better yet, He loves me while seeing it all.

He knows what makes my heart skip a beat, what makes it truly happy, what makes my anxious heart feel peace, and how to quiet my endless questions. He knows when my heart aches. He knows how to comfort me. He doesn't just tell me to figure it out. He picks up the pieces with me and helps me put them back together. He doesn't rush me. He doesn't force me to make the pieces fit; He allows me the time to slowly put them back together with the parts that have been broken for so long.

But He will not let me ignore them. He helps me. He enables me to remember that healing is part of moving forward in life but moving forward requires movement. He nudges me to keep moving and to trust that my heart won't forever ache or carry burdens that outweigh it. He offers to take the weight for me. His love soothes those places in a way I never knew was possible. No man has ever loved me that deeply. When I am lonely, He is my friend. He is always there for me, even when other people fail me. He reminds me daily that I never walk alone, even on the days it may feel like I do.

I can't sneak past him. I can't be anything but transparent with him. I am so thankful for that. He sees me when I'm angry, hormonal, irrational, sarcastic, silly, hungry, tired, ashamed, intimidated, and so much more, and he isn't scared off by any of it. He knows every part of me and still loves me all the same. That seems practically impossible to many.

It doesn't stop there. My love not only tells me that He loves me, but he goes out of his way to tell me how special I am to him. He reminds me that I am the apple of His eye, and he always will bend to listen to me; I'm the one for whom he will always care. Even in the days filled with nothing but noise and chaos, He will go out of his way to remind me of His love and how special I am to Him. When my world of busyness constantly fights to tune Him out, all I hear are the whispers of *I love you* breaking through. Whether I want to listen or not, no other man I know does that.

He says that I will forever hold His gaze. He says that everything about me is unique and beautiful- and I can be a major weirdo sometimes! He likes the way that I dance like a fool in the kitchen while cooking. He likes how I mumble the words quietly to a song when I don't know the lyrics, and then I try to make up for it by singing the words I do know loudly. He loves it all. And the best part? His eyes are set on only me. He doesn't turn his head to others. I am the one His sight is locked on. He doesn't want a knock-off; He doesn't want a fake. He wants me, the real me. Nothing less will suffice.

He tells me He wants me forever and that He refuses to share my heart. He wants all of me, every single piece of who I am. He wants every single detail, not just the beautiful pieces. He wants them all. He wants the ugly, the broken bits, the missing pieces, and even the shattered ones.

And do you know what's more insane? I choose to give myself to Him. I have decided to provide Him with every piece of me—the hidden places, the broken places, the happy places, the lonely places, and the goofy places. I give Him all of me. I have decided to follow Him through life. I prefer to trust Him and to love Him with every cell within my body. I choose Him every moment of every day. If you haven't realized it yet, He is passionately in love, and man, oh man, I am passionately in love with Him. And there is no power on earth that can separate the love that we have.

It's official. No matter who objects, no matter who tries to stand in my way, it has been decided.

I will marry *Him*.

I will marry Jesus.

You might wonder what in the world has gotten into me. Well, I am more than happy to tell you. You see, I am so in love with Jesus, and nothing that anyone can say will change my relationship with Him. It's simple. I know that marrying Jesus may sound odd, but let me paint a clearer picture so you can see what my heart is saying.

I am a super-outgoing person; I can talk to anyone, anywhere, about almost anything. Making friends was never challenging for me, but when it comes to my inner thoughts, those were always private.

We often have surface thoughts that we use in general conversation. Then we may have the more profound ideas that we crack into with closer friends. Finally, we have intimate thoughts, which I feel go back even further into the mind, and only a select few get to be a part of those conversations. Throughout my day, the intimate, deep thoughts are where my dialogue internally resides, despite my surface-level conversations. It is hard to let many people into the deeper levels because I had to feel secure enough to know they would listen to my thoughts and try to understand my heart.

Allowing people to see the surface is easy, but it is different when we must be transparent and let them into intimate, deep places. That, my friend, is scary and intimidating. I will lay those fears and intimidations aside and will let you into an intimate journey between the Lord and me. I want you to understand my journey, so I have to take you back to the very beginning, when I felt God spoke to me.

Many years ago, I felt God talk about something to my spirit that radically impacted my life. Over the past few years, I have shared it with the few people to whom I felt led, but other than that, I kept it locked away in my beautiful treasure box within my heart. I treated it like it was mine and God's beautiful little secret—until now. God put this burden on my heart; more and more stories and testimonies came up before me, and I realized this treasure that God had given me was no longer just for me. God showed me how this word not only plays out in my life but is important in others' lives as well.

I had the choice to share this, requiring me to step into a place I never had stepped—a terrifying and intimidating place for me, I might add. I wasn't sure I was ready to pour my heart and this word out for everyone to hear. But ready or not, I had two options: argue or be obedient. I decided to be obedient and listen to what God was prompting me to do. So, I began writing this book. And the question I will share, which has burdened my heart for many years is this: "Will you marry Jesus *first*?"

If you are already married, *do not* set this book down. It's intended for single people but can benefit everyone who is willing to read it with an open heart. If we are eager to learn, God will never disappoint and can use anyone. God is the master of refocusing our hearts and giving us a new perspective.

Even if this doesn't make sense to you yet, that's completely fine. Keep reading because this book includes plenty of humorous and embarrassing stories of my life, in which God has illustrated exactly what He meant in regard to marrying Him first. So, sit back in your favorite spot (if you aren't an avid reader, like my mother, then pretend that you have a place and go there), grab your favorite beverage, and read away.

This book is just the beginning for you.

Chapter One

SET A FIRE ON MY TERMS

"Set a Fire," a viral worship song by Jesus Culture, states the following: "Set a fire down in my soul that I can't contain that I can't control. I want more of you, God."[1] These were the lyrics I constantly sang to the Lord when I was a child. Even at an early age, I always meant those words. I wanted a fire for God. I yearned to burn with passion. I wanted a flame that God controlled. The reality of that song, however, never really sank in for me. I knew what I was praying for. But in another way, I didn't have the slightest clue of the extent of that prayer. It's easy to say prayers and sing songs that do not go deeper than the surface or—if we are honest—ever applying them to our own lives. Yet this song would go on to be branded within my heart, after God decided to school me with it. And this is exactly how He did it.

I'm a runner. I started running in high school after the loss of my best friend. It was my outlet. When I went for a run, I had

---

[1] Jesus Culture with Martin Smith, "Set a Fire," *Live from New York*, Columbia Records, 2012, https://youtube/OHI6DixUZwk.

music blaring in my ears. It felt like the world and all its madness was forced to be silent.

My mind has always moved at one speed—fast—but something about running outside seemed to slow my world down. Kind of an oxymoron to say running is what slows me down, but it's true. All I could hear were the sounds of my footsteps on the ground below, distant birds chirping, and the conversation I was having with God at that moment. As soon as I started running, God would always meet me; it was like our secret daily routine. There was always a sense of peaceful silence that reminded me that things would be OK, no matter what was going on in my life.

As you might imagine, I quickly became addicted to my outlet, and I have been now for many years. Nowadays, I find myself metaphorically and literally running to God. It was where I went when I was overwhelmed, scared, lonely, confused, angry, or just needed a particular time with God that day. One evening, I was finishing a rather painful run due to having taken a few days off. I stopped to feed the chickens before going inside. As I was finishing feeding them, the song "Set a Fire" came on in my headphones. God is always about timing, and man, does God know how to get our attention. During that run, my conversation with God had consisted of my telling him that I was stumped about what he wanted me to write about in this book. I heard the stillest of whispers among the chorus of the song. The Holy Spirit spoke to me and told me that the words, for many of us, should be changed from "Set a fire down in my soul,"[2] to set a fire *on my terms*, down in my soul.

I was shaken. Do you ever have those moments with God when He says one or two simple words, but they leave you completely dumbfounded? That moment was mine; I was speechless. God used this to begin to show me how often we say we want God's plan, but really, we want the plan to be on our terms. We say, "God, I want

---

[2] Jesus Culture with Martin Smith, "Set a Fire," *Live from New York*, Columbia Records, 2012, https://youtube/OHI6DixUZwk.

your perfect plan, *but* I want it by the time I'm twenty-four and done with college."

"God, I want your perfect plan, *but* I am going to date so-and-so because he seems great. I feel pretty lonely, and it's just good in the culture nowadays to keep my options open—at least until the right guy comes along."

"God, I want your perfect plan, *but* don't you think it should come this way, delivered at exactly this time, and maybe you should even simultaneously write it in the sky above? I feel that would be best."

Haven't we all been guilty of this at some point or another? It may not always have been that blatantly obvious, but I know I have been guilty of this. When did we earn the right to call the shots on God's plan? When did the prayers turn from, "God, I want your perfect will for my life, no matter what it looks like," into the following:

> Dear God,
> I want your perfect will for my life, but I'd like it on the terms listed below:
>
> 1. Exactly how I think it should look
> 2. Exactly when I think it should be
> 3. Involving the people included in my reference page
>
> By signing below, you are stating you agree to the above terms.
> Sincerely,
> Me, Your beloved child
> X _____

This is the God whose very breath formed planets, whose fingers stitched us together before the world even knew of our existence, and who sequenced each piece within our DNA to make us exactly who He intended us to be. Is God now taking orders from us? Lord help us if He is because if I call the shots, we are all in a lot of trouble, and things will get ugly quickly. I say this because I know my inabilities and limitations, yet I often find myself in a fight to try to take control from the one who molded me within His hands. I try to control how I think it should feel and look.

Here's the thing: when we dedicate and completely turn our lives over into the hands of God, we should see change begin to take place. Changes within our choices, convictions within our hearts, and spiritual fruits that begin to grow. Salvation is not meant to be built on the following mentality. "God saved me—great. Now I am going to do what I want because, thank goodness, my soul is taken care of." No, when we truly dedicate ourselves to God's plan and pick up our cross to follow Him, we opt out of the right to halt and manipulate life into what we *think* it should look like. When we choose to pursue Christ, not just because it saves our souls but because we begin to fall in love with the narrative of which we are now a part, we are forced to halt and reevaluate our lives and hearts. Trust me; I genuinely relate when I say I always am the one who wants to know how and when God's plan will play out. I constantly think up multiple narratives, imagining what it could be and when it would happen. However, the reality is that God is God, and we simply are not. We must learn to lean on Him. We must learn to relinquish our control and shred our list of terms in which God can move in our lives.

Think of how beautifully involved and intricate He has designed our lives. Not only did He create us and place into action a perfect will for us, but He still gives us freedom, even in that. God doesn't just let us be born and then wish us luck. Life isn't based on a map given to us at birth that states the divine guidelines and directions we must choose in life. We don't get a layout that tells us everything we need to know, the people we need to look for, and the time frames upon which we will set our lives. Life is not a preset game in which the Creator hopes we will follow, do well, and—if we're lucky—make it to the end. Ours is not a life disconnected from the Creator. *No.* God uses life as a magnificently orchestrated opportunity for us to grow with Him. He gives us the privilege to walk this life and choose to live it in a way that opens us to investigate and learn more about Him. We see His eternal love, mercy, and truth, which surrounds us in every moment of every day. He doesn't give a step-by-step manual, as if life is a piece of furniture from IKEA. God purposely leaves out details and specific pieces within our life puzzles. The reason is that God wants us to talk with Him for guidance. Questions are not wrong; they open us up to communication with God. God loves our willingness to come to Him with our questions, doubts, and fears. All the while we are positioning ourselves into a place of openness to recognize that life has never left His hands. He didn't lose control while we slept last night. We can rest assured in this, find peace in this, and yes, relinquish our plans to this.

At some point, we've all heard the speech about the importance of communication in a relationship. Well, let me reiterate this to you: *communication within a relationship is important.* So why do we only seem to apply this to our relationships with others? Connection best happens within the realm of communication, and in that we are invited into the beauty of seeing the other in a new light. The same is true with our relationship with God. Constant communication is vital. It is on this journey along the unknown road that God reveals Himself so profoundly—if only we will lay down our plans and timelines and open ourselves to communication with Him along the way.

If I hadn't encountered a few bumps along my journey, I would not have learned that my heavenly Father would bend down to help me up or bandage my scratched-up knee. If I never had found myself crying out to God with *no idea* of which direction to go, to follow God's will, I would have never learned the extent of God's faithfulness, even amid my lack of faith. In the moments of uncertainty, I knew that the beautiful characteristics of God were shining through with complete, unchanging certainty. It was in the journey I was taught to trust God and the truth He was stirring within me. God taught me that when my heart is in pursuit after Him, I don't have to be tormented by every choice set before me. Sometimes trust doesn't mean that the answer must be written in the sky. Sometimes it simply means trusting the answers sitting within us and recognizing that if my heart is aligned with God's, I can rest in knowing that through my choice, God spoke. I had to learn to trust I was hearing God speak to me in all parts of my life, even if it didn't look like what I expected.

For example, in the past few months, God has thrown all my plans right out the window. This has caused some chaos in my life. Because I am the ultimate planner, I was having a difficult time laying out my schedule, with no idea of where I would be in the near future. I had a concise timeline of one week to make a massive decision in my life. This one decision felt like it came with the weight of the world.

So many people had warned me against taking a semester off before starting college, saying it could lead to my never going. Those warnings—the voices of others not walking my journey—lay very heavy on me and my decision of whether I would attend college next semester. I felt like I had zero direction toward the right decision.

To many, this might not seem like a make-or-break decision, but it was for me. This one choice could cost me scholarships and put me behind on my extensive graduation plan to be a pediatrician. If I am honest, it caused me to feel like I'd failed at being the good high school graduate, doing the best with her life by following the normal path into a four-year university education. There was a lot in the balance with this one decision. So many outside conversations plagued my mind.

"You say you'll go back to school, but you won't. Not going to school is *never* the correct answer, Catie."

"You're going to ruin the opportunities for your future if you don't go by the book."

These conversations haunted me. It was like a song playing on repeat in my mind, so I dealt with it the only way I knew how—ultra-plan mode. I broke down all the questions, looking at every fine piece within this diagram. How could I make the most of this situation? Which choice seemed the most logical? Which option caused the least amount of financial stress?

I felt pressure closing in on me from every side, and I broke. I cried and cried out to God, begging for direction, begging for validation on the right choice; I didn't want to make the wrong one. I. Did. Not. Want. To. Choose. Wrong. However, looking back at the endless torment to which I opened to myself in my search for the clear answer, something stuck out to me. I believe I knew the correct answer the entire time, from the very moment the choice was presented to me, but the problem was, the correct answer was the one I did not want to hear. What did I do? I tore it apart, and I let my mind be tormented with my plans and how things were supposed to look, pushing that thought to the bottom of my brain, where I almost blinded myself to it. I just validated my torment and frustration by saying that God was silent and that I was pursuing God's will, but God was not helping me at all. Isn't it funny how we take our understanding of silence to be the absence of an answer—an answer that often has been there all along? In my case, that's what I did.

I prayed to God hundreds of times, and the 110th time, I asked God the same question: "What do I do?" I allowed myself to be angry when I was met by the same silence, I'd met the first one hundred times I prayed. The entire time, I was ignoring the small voice in my head that was giving me direction. The answer that was there within my heart just happened to be the one I refused to hear. I disregarded it and allowed the stress to build up because, I thought, God was being quiet and *had* to give me an answer—the answer that I wanted.

Multiple times within this agonizing time frame, people would say, "How come out of all the choices, you ignore the possibility of not going to school this semester?" I would respond with sharp aggravation and became defensive, stating that was not the case. My harshness became my defense for why I had a right to complain and rant because God was silent in this situation. I often would confirm to the people who pointed out this option that I was considering it, but in my heart, it didn't work with my plan, so I relentlessly prayed for God to validate the other option.

It was the one answer that kept popping into my heart, and it was the one answer that kept fueling my aggravation and torment because, ultimately, it did not work with my plan. God knew how big this choice would be for me, didn't He? If so, then surely, He knew I needed more confirmation. The words of those around me were not enough, at least not for me. When we purposely choose to ignore things and refuse to acknowledge what God has placed around us, we deliberately refuse to listen to what God is speaking at that moment. We miss the true validation that our mouths pretended to ask.

The day finally came, and I had to decide. My aggravation increased when I woke up, realizing that God had not provided me with a detailed dream during the night to show me precisely what He wanted me to do. We can laugh at this, but I feel, if we are honest, we've prayed and expected that from God during difficult times and decisions. I hoped that God would make the answer undeniable and clear as day. As the clock ticked on, my heart felt the pressure harder and harder until I thought my heart would explode from the weight. I didn't know what to do; my heart was torn. I was afraid of making the wrong choice. I was worried that this decision would mess up God's perfect plan for my life. I didn't trust myself to make any decision at that point.

Despite it all, however, I decided. I was utterly terrified, but when the dust settled, I felt such peace. I knew I'd made the right choice at that moment. I was instantly so angry for allowing myself to become tormented by a question to which I knew the answer the entire time. God wasn't silent. He'd been there and speaking the whole time, but I didn't want to hear what He had to say. I learned so much through this journey and decision. I learned to trust not only God but myself. I learned to trust that I knew God's voice enough that it didn't matter what the world was saying around it. God taught me what it felt like to trust that still, extremely small voice, and He proved Himself even more faithful, constant, and exuberant in my life than I had ever realized.

If we follow our plans for our lives, we will miss out on the incredible privilege of walking this road hand in hand with our Creator—what an honor. Like any journey you take with another, you will learn so much more about the one with whom you are journeying. The journey of our lives isn't about an unknown destination. This journey is about what it provides along the way. It gives us the ability to get to know God, to learn all about Him. The journey teaches us that God is faithful, trustworthy, caring, genuine, honest, and—most importantly—so in love with us. Our destination isn't unknown; as Christians, we know our ultimate destination. It's always about what we choose to do along the journey. We decide to make the most of it, even when we don't know what the next step holds.

This can be the scariest part—not knowing the next steps and what that will look like is very hard. My plans for my life, however, that never seemed to work out have taught me things that I didn't know about myself. Looking back, I've seen two different perspectives. The first one, for many of us, is when we refuse to follow any path other than the one, we planned ourselves. This often results in getting what we thought we wanted but longing for all the other pieces we missed along the way.

The second perspective is when we surrender to another plan— humbling ourselves to the path that can sometimes be unclear; the one that ends up with the pieces we didn't know we needed and takes us where we never had imagined to go. This results in getting all the pieces we never knew we wanted.

When we try to fit God's plan into ours, it is no longer His plan. This is not saying that having a plan for our lives is terrible, but when we refuse to be led by the Holy Spirit along the way, we push God out of the equation. It becomes the very thing we didn't want—mediocre. The best example of seeing this in our lives is the journey toward finding a significant other. Culture is a relentless ringing in the ear as it reminds us to be independent, while also subliminally reminding us how important it is not to be alone. It is essential to have intimate relationships, whether casual or committed. I'm not the only girl to face the struggles of relationship myths that culture creates while on my journey. The standards to which many people ask us to live up to are ridiculously unrealistic. Culture will shout that it supports you, but it is doing all it can to make the myths a reality and to be a driving force in your life. Let's speak about some of these, shall we?

MYTH ONE:
"Love is great, but maybe it isn't for you."

I believe God created everyone with a desire to be loved. I am not saying this is just a relational aspect but a general way of life. Not everyone will be married or even want to get married, for that matter, but we were all created with this internal dynamic—a desire to be loved, accepted, and understood. This myth, however, establishes to the people hearing it that maybe love applies to everyone except them. This everyone-but-me mentality plants seeds of doubt—doubt in who God made us to be, doubt in how God can play a part in our lives, and even doubt in understanding that maybe God is not willing to do for us what God does for others. This idea is that our worthiness defines what God will or won't do in our lives. The entire narrative of Christ is built upon a foundation of everyone being given what never is deserved within our power. Christ's grace speaks a more profound story; it speaks against the narrative that our current culture has created.

MYTH TWO:
*"Be independent. You don't need a man,
but who are you without one?"*

Isn't it interesting how culture has this funny way of telling us to be independent but simultaneously discourages anyone who longs to be with someone else? Culture creates shame around the desire to be with someone. Culture screams at us to hold our independence banner high and proud for everyone to see—don't rely on anyone—all the while using that same banner to beat us up for the embarrassing choice of being alone.

Don't become dependent. You don't need anyone in your life, but at the same time, you don't want to end up alone. Be independent but not too independent. Be separate, but don't be alone because that isn't normal. Be a strong career woman, but you must find a man. This myth stands so true and is so confusing. Am I needy and dependent on others if my heart longs to be with someone? If my heart longs to marry a man I am head over heels for, does that make me needy? No. I do not believe that the desire to have someone in our lives is wrong. I don't think that the desire to marry a godly man who loves my family and me with a beautiful passion, reflecting Christ, is bad. It's beautiful, and guess what? I can still be independent and confident in who I am and in who God has called me to be without sacrificing my commitment to another. There is never a victor in the eyes of culture. Enough is never enough. Why are we surprised by the paradoxical lies culture sells as truths?

Culture is right; I can be independent, and these past few years have shown me that I can have a career and be independent. But that doesn't mean I want to stay that way forever. Wanting a spouse doesn't make me needy or lonely. It is simply my desire to understand Christ's love in an even more intimate way through the covenant of marriage, by glimpsing into the eyes of a man who steals my breath away. If I continue to let culture bend my ideas of what my desires should and should not look like, can I look in the mirror and say that the person looking back at me is truly a reflection of Christ? If culture speaks such a counternarrative that constantly puts shame and confusion in my life, I dare say no. I'd begin to look just like everyone else, which is precisely the problem.

MYTH THREE:
"Time is ticking; better get to it."

This standard for viewing relationships is prevalent, and whether we want to admit it or not, this impacts us more than we might let on. There is a perfect plan in landing the perfect spouse, and usually, it starts something like this:

Scene: A young girl walks briskly from the library, carrying a stack of books that impedes her view of the staircase in front of her. Right as she is tripping down the first step, a strange hand grasps her wrist and catches her before she takes an inevitable and most likely severe tumble down the long flight of steps. The books fly everywhere, and as the young girl turns in relief to see what strange force caught her, she locks eyes with the most beautiful man she has ever seen. Their eyes are laser-focused on each other, their breath is shallow, and their hearts are beating like a hummingbird's wings. He smiles at her, and she smiles at him. In that moment, they both know they have found "the one." It's love at first sight.

Now, let's step out of our rom-com movie scene and back to reality for a moment, shall we? Reality is, culture has depicted and influenced our love stories for so long, and usually not very realistically. Suppose you meet your spouse on the stairway of the library—fantastic. If not, listen up because I have another myth to bust wide open: if we don't have the fairy tale meet-and-greet with our significant other, there usually are a few go-to moves to begin the hunt for the perfect one. Where do you go to find your ideal spouse? There is so much pressure, as if the timelines of our lives have multiple expiration dates.

"If you don't get married by this age, it just isn't going to happen for you." This is a lie and a very toxic one. Time does keep moving forward, but just because your story doesn't line up with everyone else's doesn't mean it's too late for love. Repeatedly, we are reminded of the myth of time and its impact on our love story.

"*So*, have you gotten yourself a fella yet? You're how old and still not married?"

"Looks like everyone in your high school graduating class is already married with kids. That must be hard."

People often say that the expectations and pressures of checking off the to-do list within an age limit do not exist; they do. If your life doesn't meet the standards of what culture says it should, you are the odd one out. Whether people admit it or not, the odds are not in your favor when it comes to the constant reminder of the nonexistent clock on your journey with God and love. Don't misinterpret my heart here; if you focus on the wrong things and get distracted by the chaos around you, you can miss opportunities that are set before you. I believe a life spent loving God and people frees us of the expectations set by others. A worldly clock, in the grand scheme of things, is meaningless. When we realize this, we will be able to rest in knowing God is faithful. God's timing is not ours, but that doesn't mean if an opportunity is missed then that's it for us. God is a God of seventy times seventy chances filled with grace. Just because we close a door does not mean God will not provide more down the hallway.

MYTH FOUR:
"Maybe you're just too picky. Settle down some. Quit expecting so much, and maybe you'll find someone."

I am *not* saying you shouldn't settle for anything less than perfect in your spouse because that is not realistic, and that is not what God calls us to do. As I have gotten older, I have come to realize something. My idea of *perfect* is constantly changing. Culture's idea of perfect is continually evolving, so how in the world am I supposed to find and maintain a relationship with someone who always fits the "perfect" mold. No one could maintain that standard. But I think it is essential to think about what you find attractive in a spouse. Sure, you can think about physical attributes, but think about what it is in a spouse that shows your heart was meant to be with that person.

For example, I love kids. My heart will forever want to work with kids. That is just how God hardwired my heart. It is not bad for me to desire a man who loves kids too. Sure, there are probably great guys who would love me well who don't like kids. But if that is my heart, and that is where I see God calling me to work and minister, then I need someone who can work and minister alongside me. Even if he doesn't work with kids, he needs a similar heart for them. Realistically, I don't see my heart deeply connecting in the holistic way God calls us to with someone who doesn't love children. Because my passion and my call are deeply connected to children, I am not willing to compromise the call God has placed on my life for someone who will only hinder my walk. I believe, no matter how unexpected or different the significant person in your life may be, it comes down to one thing: that person's heart.

We see the physical, but God sees the heart, and there is something so important about the heart, if that is what God sees us by. There are many good options out there for spouses, but I genuinely believe God offers a best. I do not think that my desire to want someone who loves kids is an unrealistic and ungodly request.

Pray about it, think about it, and decide the passions and desires that God has put within you. And then—the most challenging part—stick to them. If God brings you an amazing spouse, and you throw a God-ordained opportunity to the curb because he does not have brown hair or like dogs, you have missed the point. I am saying that having standards and desires of specific attributes for your future spouse is not bad. Don't let culture talk you into settling because not everyone meets the standards you choose to pursue.

Run full force after God, and when someone can keep up with you and your pace, that may be someone to pursue. But don't settle; the world would love nothing more than for you to settle for less than the best option.

I want the best God has for me, not just the "good option." If being labeled picky is the price tag for not settling, I am willing to pay it.

MYTH FIVE:
You should put yourself out there more.

This myth has done a number on my faith. So many times I have sat in my room, thinking that the reason I'm not married yet is because I'm not more flirtatious with random guys in the supermarket or going out to popular venues on the weekend. I am not that type of girl. I am not the party girl. I am not the late-night girl, and I don't drink. However, I am the going-hiking girl, the screaming-music-in-my-car-with-my-friends kind of girl. I am also the type of girl who spontaneously drives to Publix late at night with friends to get a new type of ice cream. That is me, so why in the world would I go to environments that are not me, hoping to find someone who has similar interests to me? It could happen, but the chances are very slim.

Even if I wanted to go out more, I work a lot, and when I am not working, I barely have time to get my generic to-do list done. I don't have endless time to do all kinds of other activities during the week. So, imagine how discouraging it is when someone says, "Maybe you just aren't putting yourself out there enough," when I barely have enough time to do things I *have* to do, let alone the things I *want* to do.

These are the types of lies that slowly begin to creep in through the discouragement: "I'm not necessarily the person to go to that place, nor do I feel comfortable there, but maybe if I did, I could miraculously meet a confident man who happens *not* to be a party boy and ends up coming with his friends." I am sure that can happen but not very often. If putting yourself "out there" compromises your morals, beliefs, and who you feel you are called to be, then do you think you will find someone who shares the same morals, beliefs, and values as you in that environment? Often, the answer is no. Stop looking for diamonds in a trash can.

Yes, we all come from different backgrounds and have different stories, and your spouse may have a past that you don't particularly expect. But God's grace and mercy extend far beyond anything our history can dredge up. If we are led to compromise in our hopeful pursuit of a spouse, we will be left disappointed with what we find. If you are looking for someone to love you and to pursue God with you, then you must trust the Holy Spirit to lead you. You must stay true to that voice, not the expectations of putting yourself "out there more." Be faithful to who God calls you to be and stand true to your beliefs, and God will take care of the rest.

It may be in an unexpected place and come in an incredible package, but I don't believe that person will be in a position of compromise. God can make beauty from our compromises, but it is our responsibility to walk the road God calls us to, which means trading our compromises for sacrificial pursuit—the pursuit of a Savior that calls us to sacrificial love and life, and that life calls us to a different narrative than just doing what we want, when we want. The person God has for us will be found in a place of promise and amid a walk driven by passion and love for an almighty God, passionately pursuing us all the while we pursue Him.

MYTH SIX:
Sex is normal. Don't complicate it.

In a culture driven by sex, this is a hard mentality to fight, especially when waiting for the right spouse to come into your life. Sex is common, and anything other than that is just weird. I am twenty-five, and at a recent doctor's visit, I had to share that I have not been, nor do I plan to be, sexually active with someone. This was immediately followed up by three different doctors asking me the same question because none of them believed I was telling the truth. Being sexually active is the norm of today. Culture makes sex seem appealing, dramatized, and casual, but God intended it for so much more.

At first, I was embarrassed that everyone thought I was lying about my sex life, but then I realized something. I made this choice with God long ago, and no one else's opinion matters. I am not pursuing their hearts; I am chasing after God's, and there is no embarrassment in the fact that I choose to wait to have sex until it is with my spouse. I will stand against culture and say that just because it is "abnormal" to you does not make it any less valuable to me. Sex truly is a beautiful and intimate act. The understanding that everyone's doing it should never be a reason to decide something in your life. There is a deep, intimate weight within sex, and that is not to be devalued. God intended it to be a beautiful, deep, and intimate connection. If our relationships in life are supposed to reflect Christ and the church, wouldn't that also speak to the topic of sex?

No matter what your road has looked like to this point, know that you are loved, valued, and created for a purpose, and nothing can take that from you. God has written it into your DNA, and it is who you are. You are God's, and God is yours. No past choices can ever change that. I speak on this topic not to bring judgment but to speak to change. Sex being common does not give justice to the intimate, sacred, and beautiful act that God designed it to be. If you find yourself feeling discouraged by the very choice of pursuing God in every aspect of your life, including sex, be encouraged. Let's be uncommon in the world's eyes together. Hold tight and remember that you will never be alone.

Let me encourage you. You are not the only one who dreads the hundreds of questions regarding your relationship status. You are not the only one who questions your choices in life up to this point regarding your relationship status and its timeline. So many of my high school friends are getting married, having kids, and buying houses. Yet that's not me—nope. I am a successful career woman who is independent and happy but who is constantly poked by society to question where I am and my timing.

As time moves forward, the myths culture presents begin to make their way into my head. Am I doing something wrong? Am I too picky? What's wrong with me? Why does everyone but me have someone?

You are not alone in this battle. These lies do more than discourage us; they plant an understanding that we are where we are because we made a mistake. That is the farthest thing from the truth. Pursuing God may not follow our timeline, as we understand it, but I genuinely believe it is not a mistake at the end of it.

Chapter Two

A FUNNY WAY OF PERSUASION

I WANT TO START WITH A VERY UNCOMMON THOUGHT: GOD IS SO funny. I feel that so many of our ideas about God are created by this image of God sitting on a heavenly throne with a serious face, brow furrowed, and his finger pointed and ready to smite whoever messes up next. I am delighted to speak against that myth and share that this specific understanding is not an accurate picture at all. When I think of my understanding of God, I picture God smiling. I imagine God laughing. I don't picture God jumping off His throne in shock from the unexpected curveball thrown His way. I see a calm, loving, and intimate God who doesn't lose control or get anxious. I see a God looking at creation and being reminded of the immense love for all of creation that He made. I see God walking amid the sin, chaos, and brokenness and still, somehow, being able to look upon the world and be reminded why He called it *good*.[3]

This, however, may not be what you've ever pictured. Maybe God was portrayed and taught to you very differently. And that's

---

[3] Genesis 1:31 (NIV).

OK. I hope that as you read, this chapter will challenge you to see God in a new way, to allow God to present Himself in a more intimate way to you. In my walk, I have been challenged countless times to step away from culture-defined views of God and just let God speak to me personally. In that, God has brought so much light and clarity to how I see Him. I've learned through that journey that God cries with me, laughs with me, and even smiles with me. I would even go as far as to say that I believe God occasionally gets a good laugh at me. I know I do.

The adventure of discovering God's personality is like meeting someone for the first time. Every time you encounter someone new, you get the beautiful opportunity to learn that person's personality; that's exciting. Each of us has been uniquely made and additionally shaped by the journey along the way. Each of us has unique characteristics, likes, and dislikes, that create us as a beautifully complex person. When we get to discover the intricate details of a person, it is something to be celebrated. We get to see a piece of this person, and in that, we get to peek at a snapshot of the intricacies of God's beautiful creation within this one person. We are presented with the opportunity to learn what makes that person smile and what breaks his or her heart; what that person's fears, dreams, passions, and goals in life are. This unknown part of the journey can be a bit scary, but the reality is, this is a beautiful and exciting part of the journey.

Our relationship with God looks remarkably similar. It can at times be a little scary when looking into the unknown, but the more you get to know God's personality, the more the worries fall to the wayside. The journey of discovering who God is reflects a romantic wooing in which you are drawn to learn about the other. Your heart longs to get to know the little things about the other. You begin to discover the little personality quirks you could not before while you were standing at a distance. God is standing in front of us, arms wide open, inviting us in. God wants us to get to know Him, ask questions, and see His personality.

It is through my choice of running into God's arms and pursuing and feeding into that relationship that I have had more than just beautiful glimpses into God's personality. I began recognizing that God has been and has continued to be faithful in my life and to those around me. God shows God's faithfulness in the most bizarre ways sometimes, and that, my friend, is just the beginning of the adventure with God.

God's love and pursuit for us is radical and adventurous. Pursuing God's heart in return is extreme and adventurous. The places you will go, the people you will encounter, and the moments you will experience are the best pieces of evidence I can provide to you. If you don't believe your journey with God can be an adventure, OK, but put that thought on the shelf and read this book. Maybe reading some of my own stories will help give you a little glimpse into just how much of an adventure your relationship with God can be. Let me tell you—despite popular belief, God is not boring. Trust me on that.

When I reflect on the understanding that God is not boring and that it is an adventure to get to know God on a deeper level, I quickly realize just how much deeper this goes. Our relationship with God mirrors what our earthly relationships should look like. It gives us a clear understanding of who God says we are, who God is to us, and how this should look in relationships with others. When we realize our value and worth in Christ, we begin to look for relationships that interlock with that understanding. It is only natural to want to know someone we care about in more profound ways. Our hearts want to know the depths of the heart of the other. Whether it is in a platonic or romantic way, our hearts naturally desire that, which leads me to conclude that one of the most beautiful parts of the journey is discovery.

Often, when we find someone special in our lives, we want to do more to make them smile. We want to discover more ways to bring joy to their lives, peace during anxiety, and love during brokenness. We want to be present in every part of their lives. We learn the ins and outs of the relationship, and we invest in it. Now, investing in someone can be the scariest part. It costs us our time when we must be intentional with the relationship. We must be willing to invest in the whole person, being available and present through the good, the bad, and the ugly.

It is the same with God. So often, we may view God as a bank teller. We go when we need to make a withdrawal. We never go to the bank just to talk. We always have a motive. Investing requires us to do more than speak words. It requires us to action, to lay down our motives for the sake of the other. That is the relationship God wants with us, intentional and investing. God doesn't want us to come to Him only when we are hurt, upset, or have nowhere else to go. God wants a relationship with us continually, in the good and the bad. That is what makes this relationship beautiful. He doesn't walk away at the first sign of trouble. He doesn't say that we have too much baggage or that we are too broken. God's heart is for us to come to Him. God wants to be there with us through it all. God desires for us to learn to laugh with Him. God wants us to see that He can be funny too—not only that, but that we can learn just as much about Him as He already knows about us.

That alone brings a comforting warmth to my heart. Better yet, one thought that is even more comforting is that I can put a smile on God's face. I, a small-town girl living in Tennessee, can bring delight and joy to the Creator of the universe. I am not even a visible speck on this great earth within our vast solar system, and I have the eye of the One who created it all. I live on the planet that scripture refers to as God's footstool. I am so small in the grand scheme of things, yet I can bring a smile to God's face. *Wow*, what a thought. It is beautiful to think that I can make God laugh or smile or that having me on his mind brings a smile to His face.

You too can make God smile. He loves you so much and delights in you. For example, please think back to a time when you and your friends or family decided to do something silly and seemingly frivolous, and it ended up in a disaster filled with an eruption of laughter. Now remember the ache in your stomach that began to build the more you laughed. Picture the joy at that moment that came in such waves that you wished you could stop laughing because the pain became more prominent amid the laughter. Yet you didn't stop laughing because the price of the pain was easily overlooked. After all, the laughter at the moment was worth it.

There is a connection in that laughter. There is beauty at that moment with the other people. You delight in the people you are with and the moment you are sharing. God does the same with us.

I feel that this accurately describes the personality I am discovering with my relationship with God. There have been so many times in my life that God has given me opportunities to glimpse deeper into Him, but it was not until later that I appreciated how funny, beautiful, and intimate God truly is. Deeper personal relationships require more transparency, so I will be honest in saying there were a few times in my journey with God when I mouthed off. I would also say there were multiple occasions when I sarcastically spoke to the Creator of the universe and told Him exactly what I thought about His plan and timing. It sounds terrible, but it's true. I had one-sided, sarcasm-filled conversations that sounded like this: "Yeah, OK, God, I would have to see twenty butterflies in one day to know that you are telling me to do that ..." Of course, I didn't expect that to happen. I'd spoken from a place of complete and total frustration, knowing the likelihood of seeing twenty butterflies would be ludicrous and seemingly impossible. It allowed me a moment of arrogance at the realization that I had made a sure bet that God would never answer.

Our extraordinary God, however, knew how to embrace me in those moments in the most humbling ways. I found myself yelling in frustration, anger, and pain, yet God responded with kindness, humility, and gentleness. God's response brought me to laughter. To be honest, I laughed until I cried because I realized the madness of it all. Even though I believed that I had somehow arrogantly stumped God with my unrealistic, genie-mentality request, God did something radical and funny. God answered.

But wait—God doesn't respond like that, right? For many religious and theologically practiced individuals, this is just a match to start a flame of debate, but it is true. Amid my mouthy and ridiculous claims, God showed up. The butterfly flew past my face within seconds of the unreasonable request leaving my mouth. Why would He answer that prayer? This response rattled me; it broke me. There I stood, speaking to God, demanding a sign that I would have sworn would not come. That way, I would have an excuse to do what I wanted to do. But what did God do? He answered with a butterfly, just like I asked.

At that moment, I realized that God has a sense of humor. He knew that I was sarcastic and mouthy at times, and He didn't condemn me or smite me down. He probably chuckled when I thought I had it all figured out. In reality, I had no idea, but even then, He sent the butterfly just because He can. He left me to respond with only repentance and laughter.

He knows that I love being able to see His sense of humor, even among my pride. He deals with me not always by reprimanding but by laughing and loving me amid it all.

Come on—you can't tell me you don't see a personality behind that! I sure do. I am not saying that, in our frustration and anger, we should always throw out genie-mentality requests to God, but who are we to say how God can and will answer? God is funny, and God can handle us—all of us. God hears all our whispered prayers and ridiculous requests in desperation. We must learn to embrace that God loves all of us, and when we walk in a relationship with God, He doesn't just want to teach us things; he wants to heal, bring peace, make us smile, and even laugh with us too. That is just who God is.

I could write many more examples of how God repeatedly responded to my ridiculous and sarcastic requests, but I would need way more than a chapter to write them all. God is not a genie in a bottle, and I completely understand that. God does not sit around, waiting to answer any frivolous wishes we may have. But I also understand that God is not above doing whatever it takes to let us know that He is with us, and He is listening, no matter how silly the prayers may seem—no matter how many times we make hollow, impossible prayers, thinking God won't answer, out of a desperate hope to validate our anger with God. God has shown me time and time again that He is listening and that He loves to speak and move in ways I would never expect.

It is in those moments that He lets us begin to peek in and see His personality in new intimate ways that we haven't before. I don't intimidate God, and neither do you. God can handle our emotions; God created them. God understands them. God delights in our coming to Him, no matter the state we may be in. God can answer in butterflies, if He so chooses.

Often in the relationships we are in, we strive to learn the deeper personality of that person. We want to see more than just the surface level that everyone else sees. We begin to dive deeper, discovering the depths of who they are as a person. We find out what upsets the person, what motivates them, the foods they hate, their favorite movie, childhood fears, hopes for the future, and what makes them laugh. That is a piece within the relationship puzzle that creates a long-lasting relationship—depth. We must step deeper and look deeper into who they are because we don't want surface level; we want all of them.

Laughter happens to be a part of my journey. I love to laugh, and I love to picture that the Creator of everything is not only watching over me but laughing too. The laughter may come when I am sarcastic and mouthy to Him. In His humorous nature, He chooses to respond to the mouthy comments I make, humbling me to the irony of it all, as I am reminded of the goodness of God continually.

Not only does God respond to my ridiculous moments, but God also does silly things just because He can. Do you want to know what I love about the silly and sarcastic ways in which God communicates with me? It feels like we are passing a beautiful secret note back and forth between us. When God does something funny, it makes my heart smile because He knows how to do things in a way that can only point to Him. He is the only one who knows my unspoken thoughts better than I do. He is the only one who knows my heart as well as I do. His speaking to me through silly heart moments and making me laugh daily reminds me of why I love Him so much. It's like a love language that only the two of us speak.

He knows my heart better than I do, so surely, it's rational to think that He would know what my heart longs for in each moment. He knows how to get me to stop everything I'm doing, look up to the sky, and say, "Very funny, God. *Very funny.*" Knowing that, I probably had been a bit goofy and said something clever, and soon after, he made me eat those words (in a good way).

God asks us to get to know Him. He died for us to be given the freedom to get to know Him intimately. God wants you to get to know Him. He wants to make you laugh and show you that He is listening in unique ways that speak directly to your heart. I'll give you one more example, for good measure. We can call this the Sunday Fiasco.

It was just like any other Sunday. I was a children's pastor at the time, so I got up, worked on my lesson plan, went to church, came home, ate lunch, and went outside to work on the farm. My family had been working on putting up some fence posts around the pasture in preparation for cattle. I was happy to help in any way needed to get my future pet cow, Daisy. I wanted her to be the pet cow that I raised from when she was young so she would know me enough that she would come when I called her name. Honestly, I had a foolproof plan.

Out of hopeful anticipation, I quickly volunteered to do anything that would bring my cow dream to reality sooner. And if that means digging post holes, so be it. However, it was while digging post holes that the Sunday fiasco quickly began. My father and I worked on the last stretch of the property, digging the deep holes, measuring to make sure they were even, checking to make sure the row was straight, and putting the heavy posts in the holes. My mother oversaw driving the truck with the posts up the hill beside my dad and me. She had the better end of the deal. My mother sat in the truck with the window down, talking to me about who knows what, while I finished one of the last few holes. As I half listened to her story, I went to put something in the back of the truck before we moved up the hill to the next spot for a post. Somehow, the timing between us was off because that's when it happened—I was pinned. Pain shot through me, nausea immediately hit me, and a burst of shock momentarily silenced me.

My toes were stuck under the tire of the truck. I tried my best to pull my foot out from underneath it, but it was lodged so far under the tire I couldn't budge it. Trying to stay calm, I yelled to my mother, "Move up or back—do something!"

"What?" she replied.

I kindly yelled just a tad louder, "*Move the truck!* I don't care how just move it. *You're on my foot!*" I tried to avoid causing any panic, fearing she'd respond by stepping on the gas and hurting it worse. But as moments ticked by and the pain grew worse, I didn't care.

Thankfully, after multiple attempts at communication, my mom realized what I was saying. My mother, being the good nurse she is, didn't panic. She slowly reversed the truck off my foot. That response was the best and most logical, right? My foot was not toward the front of the tire; it was near the back of the tire. She hadn't driven onto it when she shifted gears. The tire had rolled back onto it. So, when she tried to roll off my foot carefully, she rolled over the entire foot again with the entirety of the truck tire *again*.

At this point, with tears streaming down my face, I got into the truck and headed up to the house. What was my comfort? My comfort came from knowing that my mother held no trauma or guilt from this situation. Her nonstop laughter was *very* comforting while I had throbbing foot pain. I was constantly comforted by her words amid her laughter: "This is so dumb! How in the world did that even happen?"

And I simply responded, laughing through my tears, "I honestly have no earthly idea."

What started as a simple Sunday ended with me sitting in a recliner, listening to my mother laugh so hard that tears ran down her face, and I stared at the tire line that the truck had left on four of my toes. Once the initial pain subsided, I joined Mom in laughing at the absurdity of the situation.

The Hughes household does not quickly go to the doctor's office, so we did the usual treatment: rest, ice, elevation, and Tylenol. The rest of the night consisted of family members laughing at how it happened and at the sight of me with pillows under my tire-marked foot. I didn't find this to be as humorous at that point, but later that night, once the laughter subsided, I found myself looking at my elevated foot, asking God, "What in the world? How did this even happen?"

Isn't it just like God, though, to take something so silly and random to teach us something? Yes, believe it or not, my foot being run over had a lesson for me. As I lay in bed, thinking that I should probably try to write the book I knew I was supposed to write, my foot began to hurt a bit, and inspiration hit. Life does not go as we plan. It is filled with random things that cause pain, sit us out for a bit, or even just wholly stun us. But God is not a God of chance. Things don't just happen and take God by surprise. God knew that I would end my day with my foot up in the air because it was hurt, even though I had not planned that in my Sunday schedule. Do you want to know a piece of this funny story that I conveniently left out? I had just told God that morning that if he wanted me to write this book, then He needed to help me. I asked Him to help me to sit down and write what He had laid on my heart.

This is why I genuinely love getting to see God in deeper and deeper ways because His personality shines through. As I lay in bed, a whispered thought ran through my mind: *This seems to be a perfect time to write your book, doesn't it?* Immediately, I laughed, as the realization of my prayer and the day's events hit me like a ton of bricks. God will always provide us with the means and ability to do what He calls us to do. He sometimes finds funny ways of persuading us to do so. Now, let me clear this up—I am *not* saying that God likes to cause us pain or that He does things like this to make us do what He wants. I am just saying He makes it known when He is trying to get our attention, and He can use anything. God knew that, ultimately, it was my choice to write this book, but He also knows me. He knew that while my foot hurt in this instance, it got me exactly where I had prayed to be. He helped me to find time to work on my book. He helped me to do what He had asked me to start weeks ago. God did not persuade me out of anger or manipulation but out of love. God knows that sometimes our stubbornness brings us to a place of decision where we need a little extra creative persuasion. I could have sat back and not used my healing time to write this book, but I took advantage of the gift of time given to me and was obedient to it.

I continually fall in love with God's personality each day. God recognizes that sometimes it takes my being stuck in bed with a sore foot to get me to be obedient to do things. He knows I won't get angry with Him, and in all actuality, I have laughed about this more than anything else in a long time. I view this as just another tangible moment of God taking my prayer request, showing that He listened, and talking to me in a way that only I could understand. I love it. I love when He does that to me; it shows me just how intimate He is with me. God wants me. God wants my time. And He has such a unique and sometimes funny way of showing me His guidance for my life. Talk with God, laugh with God, and get to know Him because it is worth it.

We have to open our eyes to the evidence of His fingerprints throughout every moment of our lives. Then, maybe we can see just a glimpse of His beautiful personality shining straight on us, shining in a designated way that is designed specifically for us.

He knows you. He knows the things that make you laugh. He knows the things that help you see that He hears your prayers. He created each one of us different from the other, so doesn't it make sense that He would present Himself in a way that speaks to the very core of each individual? God is so big. Why do we put Him in a box and lock Him into being only one way? He does and will speak in many ways. We just have to be ready to listen and be open to a bit of persuasion.

Chapter Three

BOOTED UP

THE PREVIOUS CHAPTER SPOKE OF A RECENT BATTLE BETWEEN A truck tire and my foot. The truck won. God, however, gave me another beautiful glimpse at how He can work in my life in the most unexpected ways. Hold on tight; I haven't finished the story of my foot injury just yet.

My mom is a nurse, so for us to seek medical treatment means we are knocking on death's door. After a day or so passed, with her feeding me Tylenol and icing my foot and keeping it elevated, she finally decided I should go to the doctor. I felt humiliated in advance at the thought of telling the nurse what happened to my foot. I felt that saying, "My mom accidentally ran it over twice," was not a common excuse for injuries. The best way to describe my feelings is that it was similar to when I get "ignoramus" on the peg game at Cracker Barrel—utterly embarrassed.

The time had come; I was in the little walk-in clinic, and the nurse asked the reason for my visit. I took a breath and eloquently replied, "My mom ran over my foot with the truck."

The nurse gave a little laugh. "No, really, how can we help you?"

My mother and I began laughing as we both assured her that was the reason for my visit. Luckily, she had a good sense of humor because Mom and I continued to laugh as we explained the entire accident in detail. Once we convinced the nurse we were telling the truth, we all laughed about the story.

The doctor who walked in, however, did not find the story funny. The doctor was a pleasant but serious woman who only let out a slight chuckle when we told her what had happened. After a few x-rays, painful pokes around my foot, and a copay, the doctor decided I had a nasty sprain and possibly a tiny stress fracture.

I was still laughing and honestly was grateful that at least we knew the problem. But the laughter was short-lived when the nurse walked back into the room with the most hideous thing I had ever seen—a post-op shoe. It looks like an oversized shoe with a flat, hard sole, fabric or mesh sides, and adjustable straps. Do you remember those sandals that your great-grandma or grandpa wore? Now double the size, add padding, colossal Velcro straps and there you have the dreaded post-op shoe.

Given the circumstances, my response was quite mature: "Nope. I am telling you right now; I will not wear that thing!"

This made the nurse laugh and say, "It's not *that* bad."

And I laughed and said, "Just look at it!"

She suggested that I could bedazzle the shoe with stuff from Hobby Lobby, but there was no possible way to glamorize that shoe. The worst part was that I had to go to a good friend's wedding that weekend. Horror was plastered to my face at the thought of this. Across the room, however, my mother laughed until tears ran down her face. Those are the moments, my friends, when you can love someone without particularly liking them. Everyone in that clinic room shared a good laugh at the mutual understanding of the atrociousness of this shoe. But can I say that God works miracles? Because the nurse said she thought this was not the right shoe for me anyway; she excused herself to see what she could do. She returned without the ugly shoe but with a black boot, one that went from the foot to about the knee. It was not nearly as unsightly and embarrassing as that shoe, and everyone decided that with my current pain, it was the better choice. With the little dignity I had left after this fiasco, I marched out of the doctor's office, booted up.

Life doesn't always go as planned, but God always paints toward a deeper purpose in our lives, whether we can see it or not. The enemy has a clever way of blinding us to our present, to the underworking of God.

The enemy tries to blindfold our perspective of the here and now to make God's plans and work at the moment seem obsolete or invisible. When not kept in check, he uses our emotions to blind us to the situation and only see from his perspective. He loves nothing more than to take our attention away from the present.

The hidden gem within this story is this: I had recently purchased my dream vehicle, a Jeep Wrangler, all on my own. I remember praying to God to take my desire away if I wasn't meant to have one because a quality Jeep is not easily found within a limited price range. Well, God knows the desires of our hearts better than we do because after that, I could not drive anywhere—I mean, anywhere—without seeing at least five Jeep Wranglers. The logic of my mind screamed, *No! They can be costly. They can potentially break down a lot.* But my heart wanted this car so badly, and I felt that seeing the Jeeps over and over only confirmed that it was OK to desire things, and it was OK to pray to find the right one too. From that point, I knew what God was saying—if I trusted Him with what my heart desired, even with something as simple as a car, He would work it all out for me. And God did. I found the perfect Jeep within my price range. Excitedly, I bought the vehicle on a Saturday, tire incident happened on Sunday, and I was booted up by Monday.

Ironically, it was my driving foot that was hurt. The moment I saw a promise fulfilled from God that genuinely brought my heart joy, the accident happened. I laughed at how God had used this accident to speak to me, but within that same time, the enemy tried to use it to discourage me. I could not drive the Jeep that I had been waiting so long for. I knew my foot would heal, and I would drive it eventually. But isn't it just like the devil to take our joy and change our perspective for just one moment to try to take the blessing out of a promise that God fulfilled? So many times, we let the devil steal from us. He steals our joy in life, faith for the future, and hope for our present needs. How is it that God can do something amazing, yet the enemy comes in with something so small, and it completely changes our perspective?

Perspective has been my newest word, and God has taught me a lot about it in these past few years. It is so easy to turn from what is important to what is insignificant, and when we do, it belittles the things that are meant to be astronomical in our lives. Why does perspective have so much power in our lives? It is because our perspective is our compass, pointing toward the direction in which our lives will take us. Where we set our eyes determines our destination. The Bible says, "Think about the things of heaven, not on things of earth."[4]

Throughout this, I learned that even though I was in a boot, I felt more ready for battle than ever. The enemy could not steal my joy for God's promises. He made me angry, and I was not going to mope because of not being able to drive my Jeep. People of all ages are dying, hurting, and begging for people to turn their perspectives toward God. People are crying out from dark places bound by sin, begging for anyone to turn their perspectives and hear their cries. I had the promise of my Jeep parked outside. I would drive it as soon as the momentary boot was removed. The fulfillment of the promise did not change, just my perspective.

It is time for a wake-up call, my friends. It is time to boot up. As Christians, we are not called to sit around and sing "Kumbaya" until Jesus comes back. No! We are on this earth to turn every evil plan of the enemy upside down, light up the darkness, and bring

---

[4] Colossians 3:2 (NLT).

hope to those who feel hopeless. We are the hands and feet of Jesus, and we need to get moving. We don't have a moment to waste. We are coming to a time where God is telling us, His people, that we need to be ready and stay ready.

We need to have our armor on, boots tied, and swords drawn. If we slack, that does not mean the enemy does. We need to realize that God has more important things at hand, and we can't give the enemy an extra foothold in our lives. Our time is too valuable to let the enemy waste it. Our time is too important to let the enemy change our perspective on what truly matters. The enemy has stolen enough; let's not hand over our blessings too.

As a young woman patiently waiting on the one God created for her, I know it's hard. The proper perspective can be hard to hold on to when you feel time only continues to pass. It is hard to wait for God's promises. It is hard because your heart thinks that it's time, but God says it isn't yet. If we are not careful, the enemy can make us so dissatisfied that we ignore the things God is asking us to do now. Thinking ahead is not bad, but it becomes dangerous when it changes our perspective and blinds us to the present. We can make ourselves unavailable. One of the most important things to have during battle is focus, and when our focus is disrupted, the enemy will use that to his advantage. We are in the fight of our lives, and perspective is everything.

What would happen if we, as Christians, chose to trust God with our futures? What if we believe, without a doubt, that He will fulfill all His promises to us? What if we held tight to our small blessings and guarded them like jewels that remind us of God's continued faithfulness amid the arrows of doubt that the enemy points at us to detour our perspective? We could live with faith, joy, and peace, knowing that we just have to keep fighting and pushing forward, knowing that God will work out the rest.

Then we could keep our focus on the task at hand that God sets before us and do everything in our power to push back the enemy, take back the land, and reach out to those that the world says are too far gone. With warriors like that, this world would not only be on fire but would be exploding for Jesus. Scripture says that we will do even greater works than Jesus did.[5] That walk will not be easy, and it will require sacrifices from us. Jesus was the sacrificial lamb, and we, as followers, are not exempt from sacrifice.

Many times, I am reminded that the call to walk as Christ did requires something of me. It requires me to lay down my selfish desires and plans and fully surrender, totally and completely, to Jesus. We must focus on the fight at hand and quit letting the enemy misdirect our focus. Jesus is asking us to set our eyes on Him, and in turn, it will keep our eyes on the world around us in need. When we choose to have a deeper relationship with God, it causes us to see the world from a deeper perspective.

The question is, what is your perspective? Are you booted up and ready to fight? Are you alert, like the soldiers of Gideon? Those soldiers drank water with one hand to keep the other hand free, to always be prepared for the enemy. When will you get tired of seeing a hurting and dying world but do nothing about it? God is on the move, and I want to be entirely on His heels with each step He takes. I want a Jesus-minded perspective. That is the most beautiful and costly choice, but I know it is worth it. The future will come, the husband or wife will come, but what are you doing with your present?

---

[5] John 14:12 (NLT).

Chapter Four
SHADOW FRIEND

I HAVE A CAT NAMED LEO. HE IS PROBABLY THE WEIRDEST CAT THAT
I have ever owned and possibly is the weirdest cat on the face of the
earth, but I love him. A fun fact about Leo: he's deaf. He has been
ever since he was a kitten. When we first got him, we thought he
was kind of rude because he constantly ignored us. But one morning,
while he was sleeping, we began vacuuming in the same room, and
he did not wake up. We even put the vacuum near his ear, but he
continued sleeping. My family and I realized that he was deaf, and
it finally made sense as to why he never came when called and slept
through insanely loud noises; it was why we could scare him so
easily.

It may seem weird to devote a chapter in this book to my cat,
but this cat is more to me than just another pet. Leo is my proof
that God knows exactly what we need in life. My family and I lived
in a rental house for six years, from the time I was in eighth grade
until a few years after I graduated high school. The house was great,
but we were not allowed to have a pet. When I was a little girl, I

loved kittens, and I always had a pet cat when I was growing up. I loved when they would cuddle up with me at night and how they would play with me during the day. I even put my cats in my baby stroller and pushed them around the house. One of my cats would play tag with me. I loved the companionship of my cats; it was all I had ever known.

Unfortunately, as I've mentioned, when we were in the rental house, I couldn't have a pet. I held on to the fact that when God brought us the new home, he had promised us that I could get my pet. Even while trying to stay hopeful, I still felt discouraged as time ticked away, and our family home was still nowhere in sight. I hated that my new normal was *not* having a pet; it felt weird and sad—but this was where Leo came in.

On my eighteenth birthday, I got home from school to find one of the best gifts of my life. I walked in the door to find a surprise party, and as I approached my mom, the head of an orange kitten popped out from a box she was holding. I was instantly in love with this drowsy little kitten. He was so different from the cats I would usually have picked out while growing up. He was a male orange tabby. I would never have picked him on my own—I always wanted girl cats, never tabbies, and they always had to be fluffy. Yet again, God knew better because this orange tabby cat was just the medicine for my weary heart.

Only God knew that this little booger of a cat could make me so happy. He was perfect to me. Leo's fur was as soft as a rabbit. The funny thing was, he knew he was mine, and no matter where I went, he was close behind; he followed me everywhere.

Even now, he constantly keeps me on my toes with the things he does because he acts like and thinks he's a dog. I catch him drinking from the toilet, and I can get him to fetch and play tag—most cats usually don't do that. He is so different from any cat I ever had, and I love it. Unlike my other cats, he thinks he is my protector, and he made sure he doesn't miss any moments when he thinks I might need my guard cat.

In something so seemingly insignificant, like an orange tabby cat named Leo, God takes the time to teach me something. Is it not amazing how God talks to us in the strangest of ways?

One day, I was brushing my teeth in front of the bathroom mirror when the door swung open from the weight of a rather husky cat pouncing on it. Leo walked in, paid no attention to me, and wandered around as I continued brushing my teeth. The next thing I knew, he jumped up at the wall. I turned around, curious about this weird activity, and saw Leo excitedly sit down and then pounce up, swatting his paws against some invisible object. Minutes went by, and Leo continued to sit, wait, and then, suddenly, pounce.

I finally realized that he was playing with my shadow. As I had moved my toothbrush, he chased my shadow as it moved up, down, left, and right. Once I understood what he was doing, I moved my shadow around even faster, and he quickly followed suit. We played with the shadow for probably ten minutes until I realized that I would get bored with the game long before he ever would. I called it a night, and the shadow disappeared from the game as I exited the bathroom.

I did not fully realize what I had done with our quick shadow game, but after that, it didn't matter what time of day it was; if that bathroom door was open, even a crack, Leo would come in. The game had permanently affected him. I quickly grew tired of the game, and thought that after countless times of him staring at the wall with no results, he would move on, but that was not the case. I did not understand. Why did he not grow tired of waiting on the shadow? It seemed no amount of time dulled his expectation for the shadow to come again in the future. Daily his expectations led him to that bathroom wall, and daily he waited for the glimpse of movement along it. While I simply sat on the sidelines firm in my decision to let the game slowly fade from existence. However, this decision did not last. Eventually his patience and stubbornness prevailed over my own, and the shadow began to make an appearance, again.

One day, while getting ready in the bathroom, I saw Leo out

of the corner of my eye. He was just sitting and staring at the wall. His body sat motionless and his eyes laser focused as they scanned each segment of the bathroom wall for just a slight indication of his shadow friend. that moment, the Holy Spirit spoke to me and reminded me of the following scripture:

> I tell you the truth, unless you turn from your sins and become like little children, you will never get into the Kingdom of Heaven. So, anyone who becomes as humble as this little child is the greatest in the Kingdom of Heaven.[6]

Having faith like a child is imperative in our journey with God. I've mentioned that God likes to speak to me in odd ways at times, but it always makes sense at that moment. Immediately, I saw how Leo was acting. In a sense, he looked at this shadow game through the eyes of a child. His excitement never died. He knew that the bathroom wall was where he played that game. He never stopped wanting to barge into the bathroom to see if his shadow friend was there. No matter how long I didn't play the game and no matter how many times I locked him out of the bathroom, it did not matter to Leo. Any time the door was open, he immediately ran in, waiting on his friend.

In countless ways, Leo reminds me of a child. That's why I love being around him. I love kids and their unique personalities. I love being around them. They may be young, but there is a lot you can learn from a child. A child has such a simple view of life. It's beautiful. Jesus said, "I am the way, the truth, and the life. No one comes to the Father except through me."[7] Kids do not ask billions of questions with the intent to debunk intricate theological foundations, prove a point, or win a debate. Often it is the opposite. Kids have an uncanny ability to ask millions of questions, but in

[6] Matthew 18:3–4 (NLT).
[7] John 14:6 (NLT).

the end, their curiosity is often followed by simple obedience. They just choose to believe it. Children have the beautiful ability to rest in the unknowns regarding their faith. They rest in the fact that if Jesus said it, "then it must be true." It truly is that easy.

I wholly encourage you to dig deeper into the Word and what God means in it, but I also believe that there are scriptures that don't need explaining. They are simple. As we age, we tend to complicate numerous things in life, and sadly, in some cases, it's our walk with the Lord that suffers.

God is beautifully complex and mesmerizingly deep, but at the same time, He is marvelously simple. In that moment of my staring at my kooky cat, who was watching the wall for a shadow, it all made sense. Why does the essence of childhood wonder have to be separated when it comes to our relationship with the Lord? As kids, we quickly became excited, and back then, it seemed so much harder for anyone to discourage us and take the joy we carried. What if we came to God every day like Leo came to that wall? What if we came with expectancy at the arrival of His meeting us when we come to Him? He's not like the shadow on a wall that may or may not show up in our lives. He is always present. Sometimes, He may seem quiet, but it doesn't mean He's not there. Like a shadow can only be seen in certain lights, God doesn't always reveal Himself in every situation. However, He does like to leave his fingerprints all around to show He was there.

What if we lived like Leo? What if we went to God every day with childlike faith and excitement, expecting that He will always meet us? I genuinely believe it is in steps like this that we can know God on a more intimate level. God is so amazing; we will never leave His presence feeling bored, and it will only feed our hunger to keep coming back for more of Him.

He wants to be more than just the number you call when you're in trouble or when your family member is in the hospital. He wants to be your reason for waking up excited every morning. He wants to be the reason for your joy. He wants you to see Him through the eyes of a child, so you can see just how beautiful He is.

When we look at Him through a child's eyes, we find ourselves engulfed in moments of staring up at Him and realizing how small we are. We begin to truly see ourselves in comparison to the God who is returning the same beautiful gaze. We are so small, and He is so much more than we could ever express in words.

Even in that moment of feeling so small, however, you can't help but realize the love and purpose that He has for you. Each moment you spend with Him continues to mold you through the imprint that being in His presence leaves behind. This big God who created the heavens and earth and breathed out the stars in the sky[8] still looks at you and sees His most beautiful and favorite creation of all. In the presence of the Lord, all feelings of doubt, fear, and insecurity have no choice but to fall at the throne of God. It's in that moment when we can see ourselves for the first time in a new way. We begin to see through the lens of our heavenly Creator, and we see just how priceless and significant each one of us truly is in the eyes of God.

If we could grasp what God's Word says about us as if we were children, imagine how we would take away the ammunition that the enemy has had for far too long. No longer would we struggle with our identities because the Bible says we were made in God's image.[9] No longer could the enemy bring up our past because the Bible says that God has cast our sins as far as the east is from the west,[10] and if God doesn't remember our sins, then why should we?

We claim to live with childlike faith, but do we? Childlike faith is when we see that there are more complicated things that we do not understand, and that is OK because we are hungry to continue learning. When we see the complications, we still hold on to the beautifully simple truth about God and who He is. That is the perspective to which we should hold tight. We should desire to

[8] Psalm 33:6 (NIV).
[9] Genesis 1:27 (NLT).
[10] Psalm 103:12 (NLT).

know more about God but never lose our childlike wonder along the journey.

If we could allow ourselves to walk this journey with childlike faith, we would always stand amazed at our God. We would sit daily at that wall and stare for any possible sign of a shadow because it doesn't matter how many days it doesn't show up; we know that one day, it will. We would persevere through the times when God seems quiet, sitting at the wall because God says He will never leave us or forsake us.[11] He wants us to come to Him. He wants us to sit at His feet daily, to spend time with Him.

Don't let the disappointments of yesterday steal your joy and expectations of the future. No matter the difficulties that children may face in their lives; I feel that each day, they wake up with something in their spirits. Sadly, all children have not experienced the best life, but they hold on to that expectancy in their hearts—that one day, things will be different. They have faith that God is going to turn things around.

We must hold on when the enemy hits us from every direction, when our world is collapsing, when everyone is against us, and when we feel like we will break. We must persevere. We must choose to hold on to our childlike faith. Don't hand the enemy anything. We cannot give him our joy and expectations for life when rough times come. It is easier said than walked, but those times will not last forever. We cannot cheaply give up our faith during our moments of weakness in the battle. God is faithful through every struggle, no matter how they may rage around us.

I want to be like Leo. I want to live every day with a childlike expectancy in my spirit. I want to sit at the feet of Jesus and stare at Him, waiting to see when He'll show Himself and do something extraordinary. I want to pursue Him daily and never quit meeting with Him. No matter how silly I look, no matter the magnitude of people hoping I will fail, and no matter how many times I have to

---

[11] Deuteronomy 31:6 (NIV).

keep showing up to that wall, I will chase after my Creator—even if that means I sit at a blank wall for days and days, waiting for a glimpse of that beautiful shadow that I love and know will come.

> Those who live in the shelter of the Most High
> will find rest in the shadow of the Almighty.
> This I declare about the LORD:
> He alone is my refuge, my place of safety.
> He is my God, and I trust him.[12]

---

[12] Psalm 91:1–2 (NLT).

Chapter Five

TANGLED IN HEARTSTRINGS

HIKING IS ONE OF MY FAVORITE THINGS TO DO. EVER SINCE I WAS young, it has been an outlet for me. I love to climb and reach the top of a beautiful overlook and sit there in awe of how amazing my God is. In those moments, I am reminded of how big God is and just how small I am. My eyes are quickly reminded that He created these very valleys and formed these mountains. With his finger, he drew the line and looked to the water and showed the water exactly where to stop. I find myself silent at those thoughts, and I love being left speechless by God, especially since I like to talk.

Fun fact: I am the undisputed queen of hiking trail cleanliness. No matter where I am, I will clean up the trail. I will clear any blockages or hidden ambushes with seemingly no effort of my own. It's just like it finds me first. No spider web has yet to escape the mighty powers of my face. It doesn't matter what I do. Spiderwebs always seem to find a direct connection to my face while I am hiking. My family and I always find it humorous with the ridiculous amount of spiderwebs my face catches while outside- not a fun experience.

Often while hiking I even subject innocent bystanders to the wrath of the unsuspecting spiderweb. If I am going to be transparent, as I said I would be in this book, it is best to warn you now. I have moments of weakness and shear disgust, and will purposely walk slower than those around me so that they can clear the spiderwebs from the path. That is not even the worst part. Sometimes when I see someone, other than myself, swatting at an invisible spider web on their face, I chuckle. It feels like a bittersweet victory, when it is someone other than me accidentally using their face to clear the path of spiderwebs. So, if you go hiking with me, know that you have been warned and allow me to apologize ahead of time for any spiderwebs you encounter.

Apart from the random spider incidents, I must admit that I am partially at fault for the continual trauma of walking straight into a spider web. I enjoy my fair share of talking while walking through nature, and this is a significant factor in the spider web conundrum. When I am talking, I pay more attention to the person next to me than to what invisibly swings between two trees in front of me, a natural consequence. Face meets spider web; Catie swats wildly at a spider web, and then Catie continues to talk, and the cycle begins again. The only hope of indication to the presence of an upcoming spider web is the slight glimmer that shows up when the sun hits it, but do I see it? Never. I'm usually too busy being distracted and chatting. Spiders themselves, do not bother me. I just do not find joy in the magnetic draw each of their webs has to my face within the outside world.

The worst part of having a spider web in your face is the gross feeling that comes with it. If you haven't experienced it, I'm happy. It is not fun, and I wouldn't want you to share that unless, for some reason, you're hiking with me, and I happen to take a few slower steps to let you lead. Spider webs to the face make you feel weirdly defenseless. It's this almost invisible thing that suddenly engulfs your face. Once encountered, it takes only milliseconds before you quickly spit and pull at your face to remove what you cannot entirely see. The worst part for me is when I'm pulling, and it gets in my hair. It's tangled everywhere so quickly, and I'll pull at the web that I can barely see in my hair and on my face, and it's just gross. Even when you are reassured it's all off your face, it still somehow leaves a feeling that it's still there.

It's mesmerizing how something that seems so unimportant and harmless can cause numerous people to go into panic mode. The funny thing is the spider web in the pathway can be easily avoided when it is identified early enough. All it would take is a slight movement of the hand, getting a stick to knock it down, or going around it completely. However, I have realized that we often walk blindly into many things in life that God wants us to avoid because we are so distracted. Before we know it, we are panicked by this unseen thing on us; we aren't sure how to get rid of it or how we got there. Our hearts are struck with unseen panic and confusion about fixing what seems to be out of place and unwelcome.

I will admit that I was not excited to write this chapter, but I knew it was imperative to share. I have been vulnerable throughout this book, sharing my funny and embarrassing stories, but now it is time to go a bit deeper into my life and the lessons I have had to learn, even the lessons that I had to learn the hard way. I pray this helps you grow and learn from my mistakes to avoid your own.

The spider web and the enemy have something in common. The enemy lies quietly in waiting for someone who's not paying attention, who will walk straight into a tangle that has been planted. Sometimes, you can get tangled up so slowly that you don't realize it until you break free and look back at the changes it made to you and how you were blinded from seeing the truth. This happened to me.

I have never rushed into a relationship. I always wanted to ensure that I was obedient to what God had planned for my life, especially in relationships. Someone eventually came along, however, and I immediately befriended him, and it grew from there. You might not fully understand the power in words until you see them into action in your own life. And words quickly became a part of my story early on in this relationship.

People rapidly said, "This is the one you're going to marry, Catie."

"I know that you two are meant to be together."

"I think this is it, Catie."

"He's perfect for you in every way, Catie."

I would reply with a smile because it was a sweet thought, but I still was unsure what I thought. Even then, I never realized the power of those words or how they would hold to my heart, piece by piece. I genuinely started the relationship without rushing; I felt content with the journey. However, questions and words can push us out of a place of contentment and peace and into a rushed panic.

God created us with minds capable of thinking and questioning, and it is no surprise that we will have questions about our lives; that's natural. I constantly have questions regarding life, timing, and so on. But the words I allow into my heart and mind can either feed those questions and thoughts peace or feed into the rush and panic. As time continued, the words spoken to me grew more frequent, and this fed the thoughts and questions in my head as they slowly grew from peace to confusion and feeling rushed. When your spirit doesn't align with the words spoken around you, and the words people say hold more weight than the Holy Spirit within you, things get out of balance quickly. I began to panic at the question, "Is this the man you're going to marry?"

It was OK to wonder, but it was never meant to consume my mind. Life was meant to be enjoyed, not thoroughly planned out. I wanted to enjoy the journey, but the continued voices that echoed in my head kept me from doing anything but worry. I was not particularly eager to acknowledge that the wrong voices were feeding me, so I responded by trying to push future questions aside and by ignoring the chaos and the questions until later. As the journey continued, the length of the relationship grew, as did our emotions for each other.

Emotions can be very tricky. If they are not kept in check, they can silently lead us in a direction we didn't expect to go. If we are not careful, they lead our direction, instead of God leading it. We are made to have feelings, but we must be cautious because those emotions can muffle God's voice and increase our own when not kept in line with God.

I had a vigorous walk with the Lord; I didn't plan to settle in the least bit. I knew the journey would be challenging, but I believed that I could run it. My pride blinded me from seeing the risks up ahead.

When I fell, I fell hard. It wasn't a fall that instantly happened; it was gradual. Mine came slowly, like if you were skydiving and going fast, yet, at the same time, giving the feeling of being suspended in time. At that moment, you're not fully able to perceive the distance that is lessening between you and the ground. My feelings continued to grow stronger but were hidden beneath the surface, and I was unable to see that I was beginning to feel incomplete without the other person. That, my friends, is the first indicator you are going in the wrong direction, emotionally. God completes us. Yes, He made someone for us, but that person was never meant to complete us. God completes you; the person God created for you is to add extra pizzaz to who God has already called you to be.

As my emotions began to lead and not God, there were moments in my relationship that should have caused us to part ways, but I viewed them as less and less of a big deal. It all happened so gradually. I didn't realize the damage I was causing around me and within me. It didn't matter if things went bad in the relationship because my emotions were consuming so much of me that they overrode anything that the Holy Spirit was telling me.

The unhealthy relationship grew, but at the time, I felt it was never better. I look back now, clear of the confusion, and see the changes in me that took place without my seeing it. I know that I let some of the people who were important in my life be hurt by this relationship. I unconsciously ignored it. Worse, I defended the relationship instead of defending the other people it affected. As those around me began telling me of the changes they saw, I just grew angrier. The people who once said, "This man is the one, Catie," were now saying, "Catie, I don't think this is right anymore." I was so angry, hurt, and confused. I would try to take their words of caution and pray for God's wisdom, but I didn't want Him to answer. Looking back, I think I always knew the answer; I didn't want to listen.

My relationship was floating gloriously into its one-year mark, and then it happened—I hit the ground, and I hit hard. I felt like it came out of nowhere. My family decided that it was finally time to speak up about my relationship, and they did. They told me about the changes they saw and that, for the first time, it scared them. Well, of course, I didn't want to hear that. So, in my anger and confusion, I ran to the only thing I knew—my current relationship. This led to a massive blow-up; up to that point, I had never yelled at my parents.

Never in my life had I felt so confused and angry. Didn't they get it? I was supposed to marry him; it had been spoken from the start. Everyone saw it. Everyone told me from the beginning. I was in love, and this wasn't how my story was supposed to unfold. I felt that everyone else didn't understand.

After an ugly moment of screaming at my mom, I broke down. Keep in mind that I wasn't sixteen; I was an adult. The realization of that night smacked me hard. I felt my heart break as the images of me yelling at my mom replayed in my head. Where had this come from? The Catie I knew would never have done that. Sure, we had gotten into arguments before, but I never had spoken with such disrespect and anger toward her. How had my emotions become so out of whack? It was there, as I cried in the middle of my floor, that I began to realize something. I had no idea what was going on with me; I didn't know where to begin to dismantle my confused mind or what to do with all the messed-up pieces of me. I knew there was the only one who would truly understand my messy heart right then—God. Even if I did not fully understand it myself, God did. The changes I saw in myself were not pretty. I knew it was not good, and it was time to do something about that.

I was ready to listen, and I decided it was time to ask God what He thought about all of this. I realized that my emotions had gotten in the way of accepting the truth in this situation. In desperation, I prayed for the true answer, whether it was what my heart wanted to hear or not. Sometimes, it takes a vulnerable moment to say, "God, I know the answer may not be what I want, but I want what you want." The moment I stepped back from my emotions and away from people telling me how it was supposed to be, I heard God's answer as clear as day, without question. My relationship needed to end, and in that very moment, all the confusion ceased, and I knew it would be OK, somehow. The Holy Spirit whispered the truth and direction that God required of me all along; I just had to quiet my heart's emotions enough to listen.

Not long after, I ended the relationship. I physically felt like my heart had broken in two. Even though I knew it was the right thing to do, I still found myself falling into a hole over the following months. It's like I didn't know how to live without that person in my life. My happiness, comfort, and life had become so dependent on that one person. That was a new process for me to work through. My joy and fulfillment in life had never been dependent on someone other than God, and I didn't know what to do. Why was I still sad, months later? Why did I still wish things had ended differently? Why was it so hard to let this person walk out of my life? The answer was simple: I was tangled in heartstrings.

A ball of knitting yarn can be neat, but it can become a tangled mess of string over time. It requires more time to untangle it than it does to knit something with it. Heartstrings look kind of like that. A heartstring is when we tie ourselves emotionally to someone, whether we mean to or not. Our emotions and the words people say bind our hearts to others. Heartstrings come in many forms, from intimate relationships to intimate words in relationships. We can be intimate with someone without ever getting into bed with them. That's precisely what had happened to me. Numerous people told me that this was the man I would marry. Whether I thought that or not, my heart began to accept it. It was as if my heart had taken a shortcut and already had married itself to this person emotionally, without my conscious mind knowing it. My emotions and other people's words began tying me to this person even though we weren't married, and in confusion, I held the ball of yarn as it kept twisting around me.

I remember a conversation clearly; my mother and I were in the car, talking about how she saw the pit I was in and didn't know how to act around "this Catie." She wasn't used to this Catie. I told her that I didn't know this Catie, nor did I know how to stop my heart from feeling sad over something I knew was right. My emotions were overwhelming, and I didn't understand why my heart hadn't moved on.

Then my mom said she felt that I had "heartstrings" to my ex. I was confused because we had been pure in the relationship; I thought you had to be intimate in a relationship to have heartstrings. Mom explained to me that the words people spoke over me, and my own emotions made heartstrings, whether I realized it or not. When we let our hearts' emotions go to an intimate place with someone, we will begin to build heartstrings. I knew at that moment that I had some heartstrings. The thing was, I didn't know how to get rid of them—or even if I could.

One morning, I was fed up, and I cried out to God on my way to class. I was so tired of my heart controlling me, as it had been. I was tired of the erratic emotions and the girl looking back at me in the mirror, not looking like the Catie I had always been. I didn't know where to start, so I simply prayed and hoped that God would do the rest. I remember telling God how sorry I was, and I asked Him to cut any heartstrings that weren't of Him. I said to Him that I only wanted my heartstrings to be with Him.

God was my first love, and I repented of ever taking Him out of that place. I repented that I had trusted other people's words for my life over His own. At that moment, I felt a pain in my heart, and I heard the sound of a thick, stretched-out cord being cut. Something snapped, and it hurt—man, it hurt—but I knew what God had done. He cut my heartstrings. I knew it would be a continuous process and that it would take time, but at that moment on the way to school, God started me on the journey of realignment and healing. I prayed that same prayer for months as more and more emotions and heartstrings came to light. I continually had to pray that prayer until I finally felt released. It was not an easy or short process, but it was a necessary one.

Looking back, I want to kick myself for being so blind to the changes in me that took place. I had lost my confidence and boldness. Most importantly, I had, for a moment, replaced God's hand with another's. Now I could see the invisible strings that had entangled me, and it was so angering—it could have been avoided if I only had kept my eyes focused on the right thing. I had changed throughout that time, and it wasn't for the better. I had stood in pride, feeling as if nothing in life could make me stumble in my walk with the Lord. I remember my grandma constantly referencing the scripture that pride comes before a fall,[13] and I now know just how capable I am of falling. A beautiful piece to this story is the constant reminder that God does not leave when we fall. He is there to pick us up. He will use that moment to teach us.

I would never have learned the power in my words or my emotions without experiencing falling. Would I have preferred to have learned it without the fall? Absolutely. But the best part of this is that I got up stronger. It didn't happen quickly, but it happened. I walk today with a more profound strength than before. I walk with caution now, careful of with whom I share my heartstrings.

Heartstrings are not all bad, but we have to take authority and have wisdom with whom we share them. In this moment of waiting

---

[13] Proverbs 16:18 (NLT).

and pursuing God, I want it to be with Him and only Him that I share heartstrings. I want my emotions, identity, and future to be found in only Him. He is my heart's longing, and I will trust Him with my heart until the day He brings me the one He means for my heart to be tied to.

Heartstrings come quietly and are hard to get rid of. They want to entangle you and overwhelm you with emotions, causing panic. They want to blind you to the changes in your life and the voice you listen to. Who shares your heartstrings? God created our hearts; his very fingerprint is stamped on our hearts. It only makes sense that He would know best about with whom we should share our heartstrings.

If you have heartstrings from your past that still entangle and confuse you, I know someone who can cut them. Yes, the cutting hurts, but God is excellent at weeding out the things in our lives that don't need to be there. Give Him your entire heart, entrust it in His hands, and watch what He will do with it. He will guard it, honor it, and cherish it. He loves you so much and wants to make sure that you get His absolute best in life. He wants to have His own love story with you if you will let Him.

For a moment, I took my heart out of God's hands and entrusted it in the hands of another. Never again will I take my heart out of God's hands. I pray every day for more heartstrings to God, heartstrings that tie me tighter and tighter to Him; heartstrings that direct my emotions and direction in life. The feeling of aimlessly swatting at the invisible string engulfing me is gone. The only strings attached to me tie me directly to the Creator.

Listen closely because I want to make this clear. There is not a heart too messy or tied to too many others that God cannot bring back to Him. God wants your heart. He wants the broken, attached, hidden, dirty, and entangled heart that is within you. He wants to show you the difference between having a heart attached to others and having a heart attached to Him. Heartstrings form and impact us, whether we see it. Some relationships bring out things that we don't like about ourselves. Some awaken insecurities that were not present before. God wants to mold us. He wants to break down the barriers of insecurities, the less-than mentalities, and all the dirty feelings of being too far gone. God wants to remind you of just how beautiful, precious, and worthy you are of a love that surpasses your understanding. You are worth true love. You are worth more than you tie yourself to. Your past relationships and heartstrings do not have to define you. God's saving grace is not circumstantial or dependent on the person and how bad the sins are. Jesus died for anyone who slips up and walks away, no matter what. This was not an easy lesson for me; it hurt and took time.

Cleaning out messes and tangles within the heart takes time, but it is necessary for growth and healing. I don't know where you are in life, but I challenge you to ask yourself if any heartstrings withhold you from God's fullest. Who has been molding you to this point? Whose voice has reigned supreme? It's time for some growing pains. Let your heart be wholly tied up to a new kind of love, just like mine is now. I entrust my heartstrings to God, and I am proud to say that my heart is completely and totally tangled in God's heartstrings. Surprisingly, my heart has never felt freer.

Chapter Six

SINGLE AND MARRIED ALIKE

FROM THE BEGINNING OF WRITING THIS BOOK, I KNEW THAT I wanted it to speak to young women, like me, who have trusted God for the man they are going to marry. I believe this book can speak to every woman in every walk of life. Even though my heart felt compelled to write this to help other women like myself, I believe God can use this to speak to anyone, man, or woman. It speaks to people who have walked the same road I have and those who have walked a different path. This book is meant to speak to the main core of all of us and call us to account for one question: "Which relationship in my life is the most important?"

When we develop the right perspective in our everyday life, God will deal with all the rest, including relationships. All we are to do is chase after God and let Him deal with the timing of everything else. God is calling all of us back to our first love. Whether you are single or married, you can always chase after God more profoundly than before.

If you are like me, waiting for your promise of the one that God created for you, I encourage you to keep holding tight. The world would like nothing more than to make you settle short of God's plan for your life, especially when you have so many opportunities available right now. And of course, the enemy loves nothing more than to bring something before you that looks good and would satisfy for a time but would end short of God's intended design. The enemy would love to make you slip up as many times as possible before Mr. Right comes along. If you fulfill God's plan for your life, the enemy wants to scar you along the way. But even then, thank goodness that God is a redeeming God, and it doesn't matter how tattered we've been from past mistakes. God brings beauty from the deadest of places. Keep your eyes out for the counterfeits the enemy will bring you.

Imagine you were told you would be getting a gourmet meal. The chef was reportedly in the kitchen preparing it and you were simply given one task, sit and wait to be served. You are starving, and so hungry that your mouth waters at just the thought of possible food being prepared behind the kitchen doors. The loud cries from your hungry stomach make the preparation of the meal feel longer than expected. You begin to check your watch and stare at the door that seems to separate you from the food you desire. At that moment, ol' Satan waltzes in. In His hands, a beautifully laden tray of all your favorite foods; the aroma alone makes you drool. The food was not gourmet, by any means, but the longer your stomach cried out to be satisfied, the more appealing the food in front of you became. There might have been a few bad spots on the food, but nothing that couldn't be eaten around. Even with the promise of professional gourmet food being prepared in the kitchen, you could not help but to lean in with desire and consider the tray displayed before you—and then you hear it. Something louder than the growling of your belly, temptation. You suddenly find yourself encouraged to just take a bite. All the inner dialogue begins rummaging through your brain at the promised meal to come and the supposed quick solution in front of you. Hunger intensified, stomach pains seemingly unbearable, and then your mind begins to spiral. Temptation hits hard as you look at the potential answer to satisfying your hunger. Questions begin to speak loudly within your mind. "What if the promised meal would not be ready for hours? What if you just took one bite to help hold you over until the meal came? If you are so desperate for food, should you be picky, food is food, right? Besides, you have not even seen the chef. What if he is not back in the kitchen preparing gourmet food? What if the promise of a gourmet meal turns out to be a lie? What if, what if, what if?" And then, in unison with the growl of your stomach, one last thought cuts through your mind, "Might as well enjoy what you have in front of you while you can."

The inner dialogue becomes too much, and, in blind hunger, you take a bite. It tastes good, and you think to yourself, "maybe just one more bite to hold me over." However, one bite led to another, and before you know it, the pit of your stomach begins to turn and you realize that you ate almost all of it. Not long after something does not feel right, and then pangs of pain shoot through your abdomen. Confused you look closer at the food spread before you and notice what once looked appetizing is actually rotten. At that moment, the chef excitedly emerges from the kitchen, glowing with pride. Trays of beautifully unparalleled dishes are then given to you. The chef waits for you to dig in, but the rotten taste within your mouth and nausea rolling in your stomach repels you from any desire for the true food.

I get that analogy was exaggerated but hang with me. You see, the food, even though it smelled good, looked good, and may have even tasted good, was rotten. The hunger and desperation for fulfillment then blinded you to the actual state of the food. There is always a cost with the enemy. It may not show initially; as a matter a fact, it may seem great, but I promise there is always a cost. That's exactly how the enemy loves to work in our lives, especially when it comes to relationships. The enemy loves nothing more than to prey on those lonely moments that arise. He presents people to us who go to church, or they don't seem too wild. You think to yourself, *they wouldn't be a bad choice to date*, and the compromised bait continually gets thrown at you. You think that maybe you can change that person—*Oh, she doesn't share the same core values as I do. That's fine! I'm a good guy. Maybe I can change her for the better and keep things pure.*

The enemy always puts something before us that seems good to the eye. And it may satisfy those who play into it—for a moment. But how does it usually end? It ends by leaving the ones who ate the food hungrier, more broken, and feeling emptier than they were before. The cost never seems worth it in the end.

This is true in many aspects of life, especially dating. The church has some very serious conversations around dating, and I heard a lot of them. There was always one analogy, that I specifically was told, in regards to dating. The general explanation of this analogy, is as follows.

"Pretend your heart is a block of cheese." Every person to whom you gave a piece of your heart, whether it was physically or emotionally, took an individual piece of that cheese. Each encounter reflected by a piece now gone. Then, imagine when you finally find the one you want to marry, and you can offer only what you have left of that cheese. Which means that if you gave away multiple pieces through your decisions in life, all you could offer to this special person is a holey mess that was once a whole piece of cheese."

This analogy is an extremely popular one, but I cannot say that I particularly like it. Every time I heard it; my mind only ever focused on the mistakes that led to the missing pieces of cheese. I never felt truly inspired to make wise choices. I felt scared of what I would lack if I didn't. There are truths within the analogy, but when shared, the key points often lead hearers to focus on a negative approach. People often feel shame and embarrassment of offering less than desired to the one they love. This approach provides space for the enemy to beat us up with regrets or decisions made. God is not a God of shame or condemnation. Yes, there are costs to decisions made, we all know that, but I think the focus should not be our mistakes or what we lack. I think the approach to this analogy should help us to see the weight and responsibility of our choices in life that then point us to a God who is radically in love with us. Our choices may not have been the best at times, but holey cheese or not, God can work within and through it all. We will have to answer for our choices in life, that is a fact, but I find rest in one thing. There was a man that went to the cross to take the weight of all my sins, and thanks to Him, I can find forgiveness, look past the shame and choices of my past, and say, "what holes in my cheese?"

The counterfeits, schemes, and decoys of the enemy love to take more from us than we realized, and the enemy loves nothing more than to leave a mark that will linger, especially if he can't stop us altogether. The cheese analogy itself is silly, but it does make a point. Whether we like it or not, we all can attest that relationships, no matter how casual or serious, took a piece of us with them—emotionally, physically, or even those we thought were in our spiritual lives.

We may feel shame or condemnation as we begin to see how many holes we have in our lives. But there is truth and beauty in the cheese analogy if we use a different pair of lenses to view it. This, to me, is not a reminder of how much I messed up in life but a reminder that even in the places of my life that I have holes from bad choices, one thing is certain: God is a loving, merciful, redeeming, healing, and restoring God.

The enemy wants to convince you to settle on many things in life, especially in your purity with the Lord. The Lord wants a spotless bride,[14] and the enemy loves to put a strain on her if he can, and he will do so at whatever cost.

I don't know your story, nor do I know your struggles. But don't look at that cheese analogy and feel condemned. God loves you regardless of the state of your heart. Your heart is way more valuable to God than a block of Velveeta. If your path in life has left your

---

[14] Ephesians 5:27 (NLT).

heart with holes, and your emotions feel broken and scattered, guess what? Our God is a God who heals and can fill those places. Our God is a God of redemption and restoration. He came to seek and save the lost.[15] He came to restore a broken world, and He came for you, so you can know that He is the answer. He is the mender of all things broken, He is the healer of all wounds and scars, and He is the restorer of all things lost. Maybe, at this moment, you feel like you don't have much to offer the one God made for you, but God cries out to His precious children to let Him fill, heal, and restore your heart. God is the answer. Then you can offer your heart because it has been cleaned, healed, and sealed by the one who formed it in His hands.

The enemy defines you by your past, but you don't have to be defined that way. God says you are His masterpiece,[16] and when we decide who will define us, it defines our journey in this life. Stay alert because the enemy is on the prowl and wants nothing more than to trip you up, but if you keep chasing after God, He will take care of the rest.

To married people, I want to tell you that as you gaze into the eyes of the one you love, do not lose sight of the one your heart should be in love with first.

I have seen countless people who are ready to be married. They are in love, but after they marry, they put God on the back burner. Their infatuation with their new spouse takes that place in their hearts that only God should fill. Whether or not you are married to the one you waited on for years and years, we can all fall captive to this if we aren't careful.

God should always be the greatest desire in our lives; we should wake up every day, excited to speak with Him. If your relationship with the Lord is not primary in your life, it can be easy to allow your spouse to step into that place of love, excitement, and growth. Getting

---

[15] Luke 19:10 (NLT).
[16] Ephesians 2:10 (NLT).

to know and love your spouse more is excellent, but remember which relationship is vital. Which choice is genuinely your lifeline? The sad reality is, if we give God's position to our spouses, we will set in motion future problems. Our spouses cannot fill that spiritual need in our hearts. They cannot fulfill that place that wants that relationship with our Maker, the place that cries out for the purpose in this life or that place that is broken and needs healing. If we let them take that role, we will be disappointed because they cannot live up to it. Spouses can comfort us, but they can't truly heal us. Spouses can help us choose which way to go, but they cannot show us our true destiny and purpose in life. Our spirits become discontented when we expect our spouses to fill that place. Something will hunger for more, which our spouses can't give, causing more issues than anticipated. God is the only one who can genuinely do that job, and He's good at it.

Without God in the proper position, problems arise. If you were to build a house with a weak foundation, the house might not fall today, it might not fall tomorrow, but eventually, a crack will appear. Then later, more cracks will join until the house falls in on itself because of the poor foundation. How can a house stand when not given the proper foundation from the beginning?[17]

This book is meant for everyone. God is calling *all* of us back to a place of intimacy with Him, a place where He is the center of it all. He is the one around whom our lives revolve. So even if you are married to someone on this earth, it is still possible and encouraged to marry Him first. You have to refocus and run hard after God. He is worth the journey. God is a jealous God.[18] He doesn't want just a part of you; He wants all of you. He wants your whole heart. Just as you want your spouse to trust you with his or her whole heart, God wants the same from you. No one can take better care of it than He can. Put yourself back in proper alignment. Let God take the lead

---

[17] 1 Corinthians 3:11 (NLT); Matthew 7:24–27 (NLT).
[18] Exodus 34:14 (NIV).

in your life and see what He does. No longer will you be dependent on your spouse for something only God can provide.

God can come in and heal the wounds of the past, frustrations of today, and fears for tomorrow. Let Him be your first love again, and I can promise you that He will never lead you astray. Sometimes in life, when you give God the steering wheel, it feels like He doesn't know what He is doing, but when you get to the finish line, you realize He knew what He was doing all along. The moment you begin to understand the unending and amazing love that God has for you will be the moment you can genuinely love your spouse in ways you never knew existed because you now understand how to love yourself.

You can't give something to someone that you don't have. How can you truly love your spouse if you can't find love for yourself? When you spend time with your Creator and fall in love with Him, He will wipe away the stains and lies on your mirror, keeping you from truly seeing yourself the way He does. When you feel the love and truth that He offers you, you'll see He is the one your heart has been after all along. Loving, trusting, and helping other people in your life will be different because you will look from a different perspective. It won't be a job, bother, or chore. It will be something you love to do because you truly understand the love of God.

Understand that we are made in the image of God when we allow ourselves to reflect the beauty that He has placed within us. Jesus spent His entire life serving, ministering, and loving others. Jesus calls us past the religious expectations of this world into an intimate relationship with God, for our hearts to be molded after Christ.

1 Corinthians 13:12 reminds us that in life, we see only an incomplete reflection.[19] Right now, we can only see one small piece of the puzzle that God has for our lives. We can't begin to comprehend the puzzle as a whole, but when we reach the end of

---

[19] 1 Corinthians 13:12 (NLT).

this race, we will see the whole masterpiece in all its wonder. We will see the magnitude and wonder of the puzzle pieces, and we will be amazed at the difference our one piece made.

We are the body of Christ, and we all have a part to play. Without our piece of the puzzle, the masterpiece would be incomplete; it would be lacking. God knew what He was doing when He created us. He knew exactly how we would fit into His beautifully orchestrated plan, but He also knew that we couldn't do it alone, which in itself is so beautiful. The God of this universe didn't just give us lives that we work out on our own. He gave us lives that require us to get close to Him, depending on Him and chasing after Him. He wanted us to need Him, but deeper than that, He wanted us to want Him in our lives.

That concept blows my mind. The Maker of the universe wanted a deep encounter and relationship with us from the very beginning. He tore the veil so that we could step into a deeper place of intimacy with Him than ever before. We are His most extraordinary creations, and He is *so* in love with us. He is *so* in love with *you*. God reveals His love repeatedly in our lives. Even when we don't see it, it's still there. The fact that he gives us the freedom to choose whether to love Him or not shows the depth of His love for us. Can you imagine creating something great and beautiful, having great love for it, and then giving it the option not to love you back? That would be hard! Yet He knew that His love was so true, pure, and genuine that He wanted us to love Him back the same way. He didn't desire servants who were forced to love Him. He wanted a relationship that stood the test of time. He wanted a relationship that was real. He wanted a relationship that truly captured the heart of His marvelous creation. He wanted to be the one who is the apple of your eye.

I don't know where you are in life, and I don't know what struggles you have at this moment. However, there is something I do know. The Maker of the universe wants a relationship with you. That same Maker who put breath in your lungs and has you written on the palm of His hand[20] wants a relationship with you. He wants you to bring Him back into your life and let Him take control. He wants you to make Him the foundation of your home life, work life, and family life.

If things haven't been working for you, let me help you out. Often, there's a missing piece. God is the missing piece. God fills the void that you long to fill. And God is the answer to all your problems. The failing marriage; the life filled with loneliness, pain, and anger; the life filled with you settling on things you never wanted—it is missing Him.

He is the one who completes us whether we're single or married. Choosing to let Him fill that spot that's missing, however, is entirely up to you.

---

[20] Isaiah 49:16 (NLT).

Chapter Seven
THE MOSAIC PERSPECTIVE

IN EACH OF OUR LIVES, WE EXPERIENCE DEFINING MOMENTS. How we respond, grow, and move from there is a big part in molding us into who we become later in life. These moments often leave us with a choice of which path to take, and if we are honest, these often are the most challenging choices that we ever will make. When looking at which roads to take in life, we may think of a fork in the road. Realistically, choosing which side to take at the fork would be easy if we could see the destination before we began our journey—see and analyze where we want to end up and then go in that direction. It would be clear-cut. Life, however, doesn't always work that way. When we arrive at that time in our lives when we must decide which way to go, the core of who we are is challenged. We must fall back on what we know is the truth and trust that the destination will be well worth the journey.

I have dreaded writing this chapter; in fact, I wasn't going to write it at all. I thought I could write this book and use bits and pieces of what was in my heart to bypass the raw emotion of sharing my entire journey. I was hoping to provide only some highlights without revealing all the ugly. However, God had other plans and quickly confirmed to me to write this hidden-away chapter through a source who had no idea I was mulling it over in my heart. It was just confirmation of the story that God wanted me to share. This chapter is very raw for me, but there are many people who need to hear these words as well as those whose hearts need to heal. Many, including me, have or still do only see the broken, and they stand or have stood at the fork in the road, asking how they are supposed to walk through life, let alone what they are to do with their brokenness along the journey.

We often face those moments where our hearts are longing to ask God how this brokenness can become beautiful, yet at the same time, we feel too afraid to ask. There we stand, blinded by our ugly and broken hearts and unable to see anything other than a mess. I pray these words will help open the door for God's healing to flood into your life and into places within my own. So, here I go.

When I asked God how I could write about my journey through this part of my life, He took me to a mosaic window. I have always found them so beautiful, yet at the same time, they look almost impossible to make. I could not see how I could take tiny colorful shards of glass and blend and combine them perfectly to make such a remarkable picture out of them. It truly is an art form that only those who are called can ever do correctly. Each piece of glass is purposely broken to create the picture. It's insane that this type of masterpiece isn't made from perfect whole pieces. It's made from imperfections. Even better, they make their pieces into imperfections to later make them into their perfect masterpiece. It's such a beautiful process that I believe represents our relationship with the Lord so well. We all have heard that He never promised this life would be easy, but He will never give us more than we can handle. There are times, however, when we begin to question that.

I have only ever heard my heart physically crack once in my life. It sounds dramatic, but it's the truth. The loss of someone is never easy, but when it's your childhood best friend, you can feel like you lost yourself. It almost feels like a perpetual daze clouds every portion of your life. Mornings blend with the evenings, time ceases to exist, yet your heart somehow keeps beating, as the world around seems to stop—and you beg the world around you just to stop. How life continues with one less person appears to make no sense.

Christina was absolutely the best friend anyone could ask for. We were inseparable. I can still remember the first official friend picture we took together. It was on our fifth-grade school trip to Washington, DC. I was wearing a green-and-pink striped shirt, and she was wearing a navy-and-red striped shirt, and each of us had our arm around the other's shoulder as we walked the streets of Washington. We had decided, on that trip, that we would be the best of friends, and we became inseparable after that. We played the same sports, tried to take the same classes, and when you saw one of us, you would undoubtedly see the other. To this day, that disposable-camera picture with the faded colors, wrinkled edges, and sun-bleached outline remains in my car wherever I go.

We weren't like most friends; we hardly ever argued. We always got along. Friendships, however, are not always perfect. When we were sophomores in high school, we got into our first fight. This fight lasted a couple of months, and over that time, we didn't talk to each other, even though internally—as we told each other later— both of us were miserable. I didn't know how to react without my best friend by my side, and neither did she. How could people stand to fight with their friends? They were a part of so much in their lives?

Even then, my pride continued to keep in the way of my reconciling our friendship. Multiple times through those months, I found myself typing a message, only to delete it before sending. I couldn't bring myself to message; I felt so hurt, and my pride spoke so loudly. Then one day, I got a message from her. My best friend wanted to get together and talk, and I couldn't reply fast enough. My heart felt so excited because I knew that I was about to have my best friend back after many miserable months. I knew the apologies, tears, and hugs were soon to come from both sides.

When we met, both of us were astonished by how badly we had missed each other. We realized both of us had been trying to write to each other, yet kept erasing the messages, not following through in fear of rejection from the other. So much time was wasted because neither of us would reach out when the other was internally begging for it.

I remember that day so clearly. I could even point out the booth at Panera where we sat for hours that day. We laughed and cried, and we both came to the same conclusion—that we just couldn't survive without being best friends. Our lives weren't the same without each other. It seemed reasonable to assume that we would be best friends even when we were old and gray; that seemed the logical choice. We left Panera with our hearts full and happy, knowing all was right and that we were the once-in-a-lifetime best friends that were so rare to find, and nothing would ever change that.

After Panera, we headed to my house to hang out there. She left ahead of me, and I couldn't get home fast enough. My heart was so happy. My face hurt from smiling so much at the comfort of having my best friend back. As I was driving home, I ended up behind a little car that easily was going fifteen miles per hour under the speed limit on the little back road to my house. That car was driving me insane. For ten minutes, I was stuck following it. Everything within me begged for it to get out of my way so I could get home to hang out with my best friend! I felt like the driver should know how important this day was to me, yet he continued his slow speed. To my relief, the car finally turned and left me with an empty road and a heavy right foot filled with impatience to catch up with my friend.

My reaction wasn't what I had expected. I thought I would be filled with joy, but instantaneously, in the quietest voice, I heard a whisper in my heart: "She's been in a wreck." Of course, I dismissed that immediately because that was just my random mind—or maybe nothing at all. I continued to drive about a mile up the road, and when I rounded the corner, I felt a physical blanket of quiet peace drop over me, from the top of my head to the bottom of my feet. I don't know how, but I knew that was precisely what God covered me with because it was then that I saw it. There, to my left, was my best friend's little white car, beaten up and sitting in the middle of the field. It was then I heard it; my heart responded with a crack.

I immediately got out and called her family as well as mine. At that point, someone else came upon the scene and called 911. I had to muster something within, but I wasn't sure what that was. Feeling numb and weirdly calm, I walked to the car. I sat there for minutes as I held my best friend and reassured her that her family was on the way. I found myself speaking, "Hey, it's me. I am right here. I won't leave you. I am right here."

When medics arrived, the world spun in every direction. Everything was chaos, yet I was at such peace. I was surrounded, knowing I had to get out of the way soon. As I stood there, time seemed to stop. I had one minuscule moment left with my best friend, and I didn't know what to say. My mind was blanking. I knew this was serious, yet all the words and things I could have said just disappeared, leaving me with the only words I knew to say: "I love you and will see you soon," right before the medics directed me away from the car.

I rode to the hospital in complete silence, an almost numbness covering me. I didn't ask God why I wasn't angry; I just was quiet. My mind felt nothing; my heart felt nothing, and the world moving at a fast-forward pace seemed to be frozen to me. I arrived at the hospital with only the sound of my heartbeat in my ears. I was met with the news that the medics had transported her to life force, and she had already gone into emergency surgery. Crack.

We sat in the waiting room for hours, not knowing what the future held. With all the chaos, I still sat quietly. I didn't even whisper a prayer; it's like my mind couldn't work to that capacity. Others prayed, and I asked them to, but I felt like a thick gray cloud had engulfed me, and the sounds and realities from that moment seemed to disconnect from me.

Something in me was preparing me—but for what? I didn't know, but God did. Minutes turned into hours, sitting in that hospital hallway. There would be short reports but seemingly no updates. Each call would give a slight hope, ending in a painful feeling of the unknown creeping in all around. Early into the morning hours, the doctor finally called with an update, saying they were putting her in a room, and the family could see her soon—our first piece of hope.

However, minutes turned to hours between that call and the call for her family to come up. And as the time ticked, I knew something had gone wrong. Then the phone rang again, and her family went running to her room. The doctors said some complications had arisen and that she wasn't going to make it. Everyone needed to come to say their goodbyes. Crack.

My legs gave out beneath me as I watched people who were like another family to me run to say goodbye. I crumpled to the floor; it was like the last bit of physical strength in my body dissipated at that moment. I sat in silence for what felt like hours as I gave the family their time. I couldn't understand my emotions. My heart was breaking, yet all I could feel was the quiet and numbness around me. My world felt unreal, like a dream. What was reality? I couldn't tell you at that point. I didn't know what to do. My heart wanted to see my friend, yet my heart didn't want to see her that way. It was all too much to take in, and her family was in so much pain. I had nothing I could offer. I had no idea what to do.

I looked up to see her dad come sliding around the corner in a sprint, asking for me. The family wanted me upstairs. The journey to her room was the longest. My legs stood up, although my mind didn't know how they were holding my body anymore. Each step moving toward the elevator left my feet feeling as if they were filled with concrete. My ears echoed with the sound of the elevator ding and the surrounding nothingness. It felt like the elevator doors had stolen the last bit of oxygen from my lungs when they closed. Then I was there, in her room. And there she was, with her family all around. That is one picture that, no matter how hard I try, will never leave my mind. At that moment, standing by her bedside, I felt it and heard it loud and clear as the echo smashed into every fiber of me. Crack.

I don't remember if I got my mouth to open and speak words or if they were only in my head. I just remember that the room felt like it was shrinking; my breath seemed frozen in my throat, and a cold heat engulfed me. I wanted out of that room. Emotions were hitting all too fast. Reality was hitting all too fast. This was not how it was supposed to be. This was not where I was supposed to be. This was not what life was supposed to be. This was not and could not be any part of my reality.

I turned to leave without a word, and as I exited, everything around me turned to white heat, and I couldn't see much around me anymore. Tunnel vision slowly took over. Before I realized that I had left the room, I found myself in the hallway, with a few nurses ushering me to a chair outside her room. They said I was about to pass out. I couldn't control my emotions and heartache that were resounding through my entire being at that point. My body felt like a coffee mug that had the ocean poured into it, unable to withstand it and demolished by the impact. It was not long after getting my feet more solidly beneath me that I left the hospital. I stayed with her beautiful family until the final moments, but soon Christina went to be with the Lord, and I left. I was numb. In the silence of the ride home, it happened once more. It was the biggest one of all, and the sound still echoes in the pits of my heart—*crack*.

My world became foggy and distant; I didn't want to see our friends from school who wanted to meet me at the hospital. I wanted to go home. My brain fully turned off. I didn't have any more tears; blank eyes looked out the window on that car ride, with only silence filling my mind.

I slept for hours and hours when I got home, and I remember

a rush of overwhelming confusion taking over as I woke up. I kept wishing that it all had been a horrible dream, but it wasn't. I didn't know how to begin to process it. The worst part was, I wanted so desperately to be angry at God. But I couldn't. For too long, I had known that my God was good, and I might not understand this life, but God could make something beautiful. Couldn't He? I avoided friends and school for as long as possible. I never felt ready to face the reality that would smack me like a tidal wave there. I probably spoke a total of ten words within the next two weeks as I hid in the familiarity and engulfing silence of my own four walls.

Then the day came when I was forced to go back. I couldn't hide away from the world forever, but I wanted to. It didn't seem fair; my world felt demolished. How did they expect me to go back into the outside world that seemed to be continuing just fine? My heart was so torn with grief and confusion. I was in a hard place. I knew that God had a plan, yet I felt like a piece of me had died, and I didn't know how I could physically continue. I didn't know if I wanted to continue.

At the funeral, I heard it crack. In the school hallways, I heard it crack. In my classes, I heard it crack. I couldn't escape the continual sound of my heart breaking apart, piece by piece. People talk about having a broken heart, but that didn't accurately describe mine. My heart wasn't broken, like a cup that fell off the shelf. Mine was shattered. I felt like a bulldozer had run over the broken pieces of my heart until all that was left were tiny shards and the dust of what used to be something. What do you do with that? How do you begin to move forward from that? I didn't know what to do. If I wasn't crying, I was angry. Not at the world, not at the rain on the road, and not even at God; I was mad at myself. I kept thinking, *if this happened, why am I not a strong enough Christian to handle it?* God wouldn't give me more than I could handle, right? Wasn't that the famous saying? People went to God with broken hearts all the time; why was this so hard to heal? Shouldn't my heart recover faster since I knew the basics, and I knew that God was good in the midst of this horrible place? *Why wouldn't my heart stop aching?* I needed it to stop aching. I just needed it all to stop.

Grief is a powerful thing. As hard as it is, it is a necessary journey when we experience loss. Another piece to grief, however, is that when it overstays its welcome, it becomes dangerous. When allowed to stay too long, grief can suck the very life out of you, heartache after heartache, day after day. The desire to live and your purpose all too quickly will start to fade.

Healthy grief does bring us to question, *how can I move forward without this person?* Long-lasting grief pulls us to being unwilling to continue with life. I wanted to let myself grieve, but in my mind, I had too many timelines and deadlines set up to truly grieve. I felt like I should be OK by a certain point or should be "normal" by this time because I was a Christian, and I should know how to handle grief. Or so I thought. I hadn't the slightest clue. And since my method of dealing with grief was slowly allowing myself to lose hope as well as any desire for life, I did the only thing I knew to do. I did what a lot of us do; I pulled up my smiley face mask and held it over my shattered heart. Since I wasn't strong enough to deal with it like I thought I should have at that moment, I faked it. I didn't allow myself the process of healthy grieving, so I inadvertently allowed it to make a home in and stay in my heart.

Days turned into weeks, and soon weeks turned into months, and somehow time just kept ticking on, just like it always seemed to do. One day, months later, I had a wake-up call. While at a women's retreat with my church, one of the women began praying with me. I don't remember my prayer at that moment, but I remember hers. Her words echoed through my head: "Catie, you *did not* die in that car wreck." I had been telling the Lord that I wished he had taken me too because my heart couldn't handle this pain. I was broken, I was done, and I could not fake it. I couldn't be strong like I thought I was supposed to be, and I was sorry if I failed as a Christian because of it.

I just didn't want to do anything anymore, and the dreams that once drove me were a distant memory. But when those words hit my ears— "Catie, you *did not* die in that car wreck"—I felt as if physical electric paddles hit my chest, and before I knew it, the current swooped through my body, and I heard the shock hit my heart. For the first time in a long time, I felt my heartbeat. For the first time in a long time, I could hear my heartbeats. I could feel the air filling my lungs, not being sucked out of them. I felt life again. I realized it wasn't just Christina that I buried that day; I felt like I had been buried too, and I was living as if I had. They had spiritually buried Catie too. I will repeat it: grief is necessary. The Bible even says that there is a time for it, but God doesn't stop there. Scripture goes on to say that there will also be a time for dancing.

At some point, there is a transition. At some point, we cannot stay in that place anymore.

When we stay in that place of grief, we cannot walk out of what God has called us to. When grief overstays its welcome, we begin spiritually cementing our place to that point in time, from which we feel we cannot move. How can we continue to move past those moments? Life after someone's death doesn't feel possible at that moment. However, God doesn't say life is easy, but with God, it is possible.

We must choose how we will handle these moments in life; we must decide which way down the forked road we will go. I turned to God because I knew that if anyone could take the fragmented pieces of my completely shattered heart, it was Him. I was not doing any good with it; I felt like I only seemed to get worse. The longer it took me to realize I wasn't strong enough to handle this, the more my life seemed to turn grayer and grayer.

I remember saying to God that I wanted to be angry at Him; I wanted someone to blame, but my heart knew the truth. My God had proven Himself to be good, faithful, loving, and so much more, countless times before this moment. He hadn't changed now. God never said I had to be strong to walk through this life. God tells us to let Him walk this life with us. He will be strong in my weakness. I crawled into His arms and showed how broken I indeed was, even though He already knew. His arms stretched wide in compassion and grace to a broken little girl who cried out and told an all-knowing God everything, and it helped me. Then I asked Him for help in harder places. I asked God to help me give grief a long overdue eviction notice. I didn't want to be spiritually dead, and I needed help to begin life again. He had me here for a reason, broken or not. I wanted to do all I could with this life He had given me.

It took time; it took a lot of time. It took repeated days of me forcing myself to evict the grief that no longer could hold residency in my heart. It took time for life to begin to feel like it made sense again. But with each step forward, I stepped deeper and deeper into the calling God had for me. We cannot choose how our lives will play out, but we can choose how we walk out our lives after those moments. My fork in the road wasn't obvious, but I knew the end results. I could have chosen one way and could have been angry with God. I could have done what many have done and quit caring—live my life the way I wanted to and not care about the results in the end; worry only for myself and turn from the God I'd known my entire life. I could have chosen to let the enemy's lies set in and fully take root. I could have chosen to believe that God wasn't who He said He was. I could have built my theology and belief in God based on the lies that "God doesn't care. How could a loving God let this happen? What's the point of living?" Or I could choose the second path—the path that would bring me to the conclusion that I might not always understand God or why life takes us on these paths, but I could come to the understanding that God is good, even when life isn't. I could understand that He loves us so much and wants us to live our lives to the full potential of His calling, and that calling doesn't change because of our heartbreak.

I am beginning to believe that the beauty of our calling can take the deepest root amid the ugliest pain in our journeys. The second path may require us to walk through challenging times, but it also reminds us that God never leaves us to walk it alone. This path has seen a plethora of tears, but it has also seen a harvest beyond anything I could imagine. It is on this path that perseverance is built. It is hard to choose to keep chasing God when all we want to do is quit, scream at God, or even blame God, especially when we have shattered hearts, and we don't feel like our hearts could ever be put back together the same.

The reality is that our hearts can't be put back together the same. The trials are not something we long for, but the response to them influences who we become. The steps we choose to take today will echo into the future. How we decide to take the hard times, pain, and brokenness will affect the man or woman we are called to be. Life is so beautiful, but we would never fully appreciate the beauty all around us without the pain and ugly things. We better understand the flower that pops up in spring when all we have seen is dead leaves, snow, empty trees, and gray skies. We appreciate life and time more when we realize we can't orchestrate it. We must live in this moment. We have no choice but to be all that God has called us to be right now, in the present. We can't appreciate that our God is truly a healer unless we open ourselves to let Him heal our shattered places. Where are your shattered places?

Not a day goes by that I don't miss Christina. I cried just today at the thought of my beautiful friend. But we must always look forward to what God has in store because we have a life to live now, at this moment. One day, I will see her again, and I've already propositioned God into putting her mansion beside mine in heaven. But until that day, I choose to live. I choose to take the fork in the road that trusts God to help me. I choose the fork in that road that says He will hold me when I am broken, give me strength when I am weary, and be a friend who sticks closer than a brother.

I don't know where you are in life or the pain you have gone through, but God does. Hold tight to Him, the one who sees your broken and shattered pieces, because He has a plan for them. God doesn't leave us broken. Like in mosaic windows, the maker doesn't leave the shattered window pieces spread across his workbench. He takes the pieces, perfectly aligns them, and places them into the exact place to complete the picture. The beauty is hard to see when looking at only one broken piece or even multiple scattered pieces, yet once each piece is connected to make the whole, it seems as if this broken piece of art was never more perfect. God can and will take our broken and shattered places and, piece by piece, place our hearts back in a new way, a never-before-seen way.

Light can shine through that mosaic heart like never before—the awe-inspiring artwork of a Maker who made our brokenness into beauty. I am a true testament. My name is Catie, and I have a mosaic heart, one that was shattered beyond what I thought repairable but was perfectly placed back together into a heart that beats with more fervor after God and who He has called me to be.

My perspective has changed; no longer do I stare at the shattered pieces and see what used to be that is now unable to be. No, I wait in hope and anticipation as I sit back and watch the craftsman work. I sit back as I watch the formation of all the masterpieces God can and will make out of those pieces if He's only allowed.

> Now we see things imperfectly, like puzzling reflections in a mirror, but then we will see everything with perfect clarity. All that I know now is partial and incomplete, but then I will know everything completely, just as God knows me completely.[21]

---

[21] 1 Corinthians 13:12 (NLT).

Chapter Eight

WHAT'S YOUR FAIRY TALE ENDING?

WHAT'S YOUR STORY LOOK LIKE? WHAT IS IT THAT YOU DREAM OF? Maybe it isn't a man who wears tights and comes riding in on a white horse to save the day, but we all envision something. I picture the man being funny and enjoying hiking with me. That's where I find my heart drawn.

I think most of us have watched the sweet princess movies growing up and wished for a love like that, as silly as it may seem. The funny part is that we can look at any princess love story and call the ending before it happens. They usually are the same. The books and fairy tales we grew up reading end with a climactic scene of the prince running to save the day. Whether that's breaking the curse with true love's kiss, climbing towers, or fighting dragons, they all end with a pen writing down these simple words: "And they lived happily ever after." The credits' role, and we are left happy and wishing we could watch the rest of the love story unfold. I know I always wanted more. I felt like the rest of the story was just as important, and I felt sad that the story ended. We live into other people's stories, or for clearer understanding, we live into other pretend people's stories.

We must realize that we may not want the love scene of the man riding in on a white horse with matching tights into our dangerous situation and saving us from the evil dragon. Come on; I will be the first to admit that tights would be a quick turn-off for me. But I will say that my heart feeds on those stories because it craves the same kind of sacrificial love. We all want to be loved deeply. We want someone to see the real us and love us for exactly who we are and know they would fight with us and for us. We want the fairy tale ending, even if we don't want to admit it.

The truth of the matter is that our stories are way better than any cartoon romance we grew up with. Our author doesn't write the same story with a different princess and villain. We don't have to live out our hopes and dreams through cartoon love stories. We serve a God who uniquely writes stories. Not one is the same. We have a God who writes our stories as uniquely fitted for us. And the even better part is that we have a say in what that looks like and even how it ends.

Free will is the scariest yet most beautiful thing about this life. God created a world full of people He loves so much, but He still gives them the ability to choose Him or not. He gives all of us the ability to choose our stories. No matter which direction you choose, His fingerprints will be all over it. You can't escape the beauty marks that God has all around us. There is no place too dark, dirty, or scary that God can't bring you out or, better yet, meet you within. He is not afraid of the mess that might be in that tower. He is not scared of the scars that are under the sleeves of that gown. He is not afraid of the past that holds onto you like a backpack.

He is in love with you, and nothing will stand in the way of His love for you. If all we got from this life was God and nothing else, it would still be worth it. He is our everything. He is our reason for living. He has a plan for every one of us that only we can fulfill.

Many years ago, I heard the most beautifully articulated view on purpose within our lives. I can't remember who said it, but I can describe the gist of what was shared. The main point was that once we understand the purpose that God has for our lives, we will never wish to be anyone else. We will know that only we can do exactly what God has called us to do. He fulfills the deepest parts of us and brings out the deepest joys within us.

He knows the desires of our hearts. We must trust Him with every piece of our lives, not just part of it. His plan will be amazing. We often are so worried about getting all the things we want out of life that we don't have time for God. But He is saying that if we chase after Him in relentless pursuit, He will bring everything that we never even realized we always wanted. And I can promise you one thing: His plan is better than ours.

My prayer for this book is that it has deepened your understanding of who God is. I pray that you catch glimpses of His beautiful personality and character throughout the stories of my life. He is always present and is the best adventure you could ever have. Love for you pours from every piece of Him. I pray that you see His fingerprints all around you and that you see Him for who He wants to be in your life.

What will your fairy tale ending be? You get to decide who is at the end of your aisle.

Chapter Nine

WHO'S AT THE END OF YOUR AISLE?

My reason for writing this book goes back to a dream I had one night. Have you ever had a moment that shakes you to your core and forever imprints on your brain and heart? This was mine.

I had the dream sometime toward the end of high school. I can remember every detail of this dream because it felt *so* real. I felt more emotion than I felt when I was awake in real life. It was more real in this dream than it ever had been before.

In the dream, it was my wedding day. I felt a feeling in my heart that at any moment, I would explode from happiness, and the butterflies in my stomach continued to converse with my heartbeat. The smile I had on my face was so big and genuine that it began to hurt. I wore a princess dress—the type of dress I always found beautiful. My hair was half up and half down, just like I always wanted. To my right was my dad, whose arm was intertwined in mine. His smile was pure joy, as his eyes were wet and brimming with tears.

We were in a church filled with people in multitudes of rows on both sides. They were blurry, but I knew they all shared in my joy. Then we began walking down the carpeted aisle toward a man standing with the preacher. The face of the man with the preacher was blurry, but it didn't matter. I knew the man; I knew he was the one for whom I had waited. This man was the reason I had saved myself. He was the one who God made when He thought of me. Even though his face was blurred, everything about him was so clear. He was exploding with joy and couldn't stop smiling. He was handsome, and I knew he shared the same heart that I had.

I felt as if my smile got bigger with each step I took toward him. As soon as I stepped up to the altar with my dad, the man standing at the altar was no longer blurry. In an instant, I realized who this man was—He was Jesus, and He was now standing before me. He was not blurry at all. Everything about Him was beautiful and true. My joy did not change, but I was unsure at first what He wanted. He stood where my husband would stand, with passion yet gentleness in His eyes. He reached a hand out to me. For a moment, it was as if it was just Him and me at the end of that aisle. He smiled at me and wanted to know if I would marry Him first. That question went from the surface of my ears and penetrated every part of me, and in that instant, I understood everything behind those five words. Without any hesitation, I smiled, put my hand in His, and replied, "Yes."

When I said yes, a smile lit up Jesus's face, and in that same instant, He was gone. Now another man stood before me, with my hand in his hand. It was no longer Jesus, and his face was blurry. But I still knew this man; I felt like I knew him better than anyone on this earth. He was the man God had created for me to marry. He was my husband. Then I woke up.

This dream felt seared in my heart. I didn't need God to explain what He was saying to me; I knew. Every detail of that dream was so beautifully orchestrated, and I found myself amazed at the details, even down to the dress and hairstyle being what I always had wanted as a little girl. God made clear to me three things in those few moments of that dream.

First, He reiterated to me that He knows my heart's desires. He knows me better than I know myself. He knows my dream wedding dress and how I want to wear my hair. He knows how important my wedding day will be to me because I have chosen to save myself for the man I marry. He understands that the road of waiting can get hard and lonely. He knows everything.

Second, He made it clear that this day was meant to carry *true joy*. I got a glimpse of the emotions I will feel on that day. I knew that every tear I cried, every lonely night, every hope of the enemy for me to fail, every attack from the enemy, and every moment I was tired but continued to fight was worth it. The entire journey up to here was all worth it. The joy that I felt brought a beautiful perspective. I knew the road I had chosen to walk. I knew it would not be easy in today's world, but God honors those who run after Him first. God asks us to trust Him on this journey. I couldn't see the face of my husband, but I knew God was saying that if I trusted in Him, it would be worth the wait. The Lord, I am sure, also knew that if I'd seen my husband's face in the dream, I couldn't have handled it. Because let's be honest; I am still human. Even if I tried not to see someone who resembled him, it would probably distract me quite a bit on this journey. Anytime God has shown me glimpses of my husband and me, He never lets me see his face. It's always blurry. God knows me very well.

The final point in my dream was that God wanted me to make Him most important in my life. I have heard many people say that we need to "date" God and get to know Him. In this dream, God was asking something deeper of His bride—a place that goes beyond dating, pursuing, and getting to know each other better. God wants that, but He is not satisfied with that. He wants intimacy with us that lasts; He wants a relationship that joins two together for better or worse. He wants a marriage. He wants a committed relationship that we fight for daily, one that goes deeper than knowing the basics of one another.

The relationship He wants is much more than that. He wants a forever with us. He wants each of us to spend every day getting to know Him more and more, which results in our falling deeper in love with Him. Our desire can then change from just a pursuit to know the basics of God and a noncommittal dating relationship that can be on and off like a light switch. He wants a lasting relationship, one that never ends and always continues to grow.

Marriage is much deeper than dating. The heart is so much more involved when you marry someone. The depths of intimacy that your heart allows are the depths that only you decide. Love is a powerful thing, and when you can understand how deep God's love goes, you will never want to stop going deeper with Him. You will taste and see that He is good,[22] and then I pray that you will be so addicted to Him that all you will want is more and more of what God freely offers.

God has no limits, so this is not a relationship that will leave you unsatisfied. There is always more available when it comes to your relationship with God. Just like a spouse, the more you love being around them, the more time you want to spend with them. I want my relationship with the Lord to be permanent and lifelong. I want to spend each day trusting in Him and getting to know Him more and more. I want to allow him daily to show me how to reach others and be more discerning of Him and what the Holy Spirit speaks to my heart. I want to be someone so in tune with God that my focus is in the here and now with Him. I desire that I will fall more passionately in love with Him daily. I hope for my heart to move when the Holy Spirit says to move. I don't want to waste a single moment of this life being caught up in my plans. I want to be so consumed by my relationship with God that I don't have time to carry the burdens of this life. I can trust that this relationship is a journey with a magical ending.

I choose to run after God with all I have. Just as a spouse must choose to trust the other, I choose to trust that in the right timing

---

22 Psalm 34:8 (NLT).

and by His plan, God will beautifully bring the pieces of my life together into His fantastic masterpiece. All I must do is chase after Him and, in His timing, run straight into my destiny that He has planned for me.

The choice is ultimately yours. This life is meant to be lived with passion. I pray you choose to live that way. I pray that you decide to run with love so deep for God that it floods into every aspect of your life. When intimacy with God runs deep, passion for Him will overflow in every part of your life as the outcome.

The Lord told me to write this book because I knew this dream was not just meant for me. Whether you fully understand or not, the Maker of the universe, the one who blew breath into your lungs, loves you so much. He wants a lasting and intimate relationship with you. His heart longs for you and wants to show you so many things during this life. Your choice in pursuing Him opens you up to endless encounters with Him. When you put Jesus first, everything else in your life will connect in such a beautiful way. He is the foundation that will never fail. He helps you see the beauty that can come from ashes, the laughter in the random moments, the freedom from heartstrings that bind you, the freedom from your plans in life, and the joy of the intimacy in the journey. It all starts when He is put in His rightful place in your life—first.

What do you have to lose? Give Him a shot, get to know Him, and just see where the road goes from there. I can promise you this: a journey with Him is worth it all. Give Him the reins for a while and see the difference it makes in your life when you no longer have to worry or plan it all out. You can just run after Him, and He will take care of the rest.

I will leave you with one question:

Will you marry Jesus first?